RIDING OUTSIDE THE LINES

ALSO BY JOE KURMASKIE

Metal Cowboy:
Tales from the Road Less Pedaled

RIDING OUTSIDE THE LINES

International Incidents and Other Misadventures with the Metal Cowboy

JOE KURMASKIE

THREE RIVERS PRESS
NEW YORK

Published by Three Rivers Press, New York, New York.
Member of the Crown Publishing Group, a division
of Random House, Inc.
www.randomhouse.com

THREE RIVERS PRESS and the tugboat design are
registered trademarks of Random House, Inc.

Printed in the United States of America

Design by Karen Minster

Library of Congress Cataloging-in-Publication Data
Kurmaskie, Joe.
Riding outside the lines : international incidents and
other misadventures with the metal cowboy / Joe
Kurmaskie.—1st ed.
p. cm.
1. Kurmaskie, Joe. 2. Cyclists—United States—
Biography. 3. Journalists—United States—Biography.
I. Title.
GV1051.K87 A33 2003
796.2'092—dc21
2002012316

ISBN 1-4000-4798-6
10 9 8 7 6 5 4 3 2 1
First Edition

For my father—
who gave without question
and showed me that
a good man is a rare gift
to the world.

ACKNOWLEDGMENTS

If not for the kindness of strangers and quite a few friends and family members, my life would feel more like a Kafka novel than a Jimmy Buffett song. I'd like to thank my best gal, Beth, for her infinite patience and constant support. Quinn and Lorenzo, you boys are my reward. Mom for always championing the creative spirit in all of us. Jen, Tim, and Dan, there's no bond like the ones between siblings, I love you guys. The Biaginis for taking me into your family with such open arms for more than a decade now. To my pal Christopher Swain for his humor, work effort, and for swimming the river so the rest of us may some day drink from it without growing a third eye. Matt and Emily Siegel—let's see some little Siegels soon. Jay Atkinson: your friendship, help, and dent-headed sage advice (you are my elder, you know) made that plate of carp we had to choke down worth it. See you at the Hawaii House. A special thank-you to my editor, Carrie Thornton; you turned what could have been a tug-of-war into a twenty-four-hour party. Thanks for really getting it, so much so that you could make it better. Tim Roethgen is a godlike creature towering above the rest of the publicity world. All the editors at magazines and newspapers who keep publishing my dispatches, diatribes, and bits of inspired mayhem, *gracias*. And for the many I've missed with this little shout out, it's been said that we aren't here for a long time, so we'd do well to make it a good time.

Thanks for doing just that throughout my life.

CONTENTS

I was on summer vacation for about . . .
twenty years.
JAY ADAMS, *DOGTOWN AND Z-BOYS*

Anyone named Picasso is excused.
The rest of you need to stay inside the lines.
OVERHEARD IN A SECOND-GRADE ART CLASS

It's not a daydream
if you decide to make it your life.
TRAIN

RIDING OUTSIDE THE LINES

Hey, you wanna go for a ride?

Forget about the latest gear and quit worrying if you'll have enough power in your hindquarters to keep up. It's not a race. All I ask is that you want to *go* somewhere. Really get out of town. Destination? Well, that's not so important either, as long as it's a decent clip from the Interstate.

See, my adventures here in *Riding Outside the Lines* are about taking chances, heading into the day wide open and leaving all the trappings of your adult life behind for a few miles. Riding literary shotgun with me is similar to boarding one of those coasters that blows through town as part of a ramshackle traveling carnival—you want to buy a ticket, but just look at the thing! Will I live to tell the tale if I give it a spin? Still, you gotta have a little fun in this life. I can't promise you a smooth ride, but if you're looking for safe and predictable, Disney World's always open—or you could just read another John Grisham novel.

But, there is some method to this rolling mayhem. Granted, in one story we're pedaling to traditional Highland Games in Perth, Australia, to retrieve my wallet, and the next thing you know we're battling wind, rain, and eardrum damage across Ireland in hot pursuit of a squad of winsome

1

young female bagpipe players. What strings these stories together and those in my first book, *Metal Cowboy,* is pacing. I structure my collections to feel like a complete ride. Sometimes you're barreling downhill and life couldn't get any better, and before you know it you have to gut it out and climb over the top to avoid a heap of pain. Along the way we'll chuckle, bleed, and eat some barely identifiable grub. It's not obvious, mind you, but by the last page of *Riding Outside the Lines* we'll know we rode this one together.

Why a bicycle and not, say, a camel, ultralight or rickshaw? Simple. Spitting, heights, and I only run if the police are chasing me.

Too many travel narratives beat up the reader with the premise that it's all about the journey. And you know what? They're right. But you can't package that journey into a neat little box and tell people this is what you should do to have an authentic experience. It's not what you'll find in my books. When we leave the front door, anything can happen. As long as we pedal with some interesting folk and have a few off-the-hook moments along the way, does it really matter if we know where we're gonna sleep at night? If it did, we might miss out on bunking at sheep ranches on New Zealand's South Island, bumping along in the back of a jeep beside Mexican freedom fighters, or bedding down in five-hundred-year-old castles.

I recently spotted a self-help book at the grocery store called *Teach Yourself How to Dream: A Practical Guide.* This made me laugh loud, long and hard, until security moved in. Are we so hung up on making everything in life deliberate that we need someone else to teach us how to do what comes naturally just by closing our eyes? I hope not.

So close your eyes, and let's go for a ride.

ON YERE BIKE

I took a place in one of the booths near the door, intent on ordering something warm. A traditional pub: darts, fireplace, and a long bar already crowded with Irishmen pouring that dark mother's milk down their throats. It might have been about ten in the morning. The joint was rowdy enough by anyone's standards, on a weekday no less, that I wanted to hang around and see how it ended. But this was only meant as a brief pit stop before pedaling back into the breach.

The rain hadn't really stopped lashing since before breakfast, and the wind, like the higher math I so loathed back in school, was a constant. Seeing as I'd volunteered to bicycle around my ancestral homeland, I felt duty-bound to offer casual disregard in the face of the harshest weather. Given my pitiful state after less than a week of sloshing about country roads, my relatives, were they still aboveground, would certainly have shunned me. Or, at the very least, they would have called me cruel names, like *plonker* and *wank,* before letting me buy them a pint.

I was too cold to shed my blue Gore-Tex shell and pants. When I glanced in the mirror behind the bar the image staring back resembled a bulky blueberry as painted by Keith Haring—practically glowing. Had my rain suit always been so loud, or did the sea of muted jackets surrounding me raise its reflective properties to clownlike proportions? One of the patrons, about my age, noticed me noticing myself and leaned over. "What do ya call an Irishman in one of them spiffy rain suits?"

I shrugged.

"You call him a tourist. We wouldn't be caught dead wearing that shite."

He smiled, a good-natured grin. The rest of the pub must have been listening, because the place broke into hearty laughter. I joined in. What the hell—it was a good joke even if I happened to be the punch line.

Clearly, my reaction suited them, because an open stool quickly appeared and handshakes were exchanged. The comedian's name turned out to be Brian, and his friends were damn near everyone in the place. When the second round arrived I realized a sip too late that I was participating in my first genuine "session." To leave at this point would have been beyond rude. Having heard that these things could last indefinitely, I ordered myself a substantial amount of grub, hoping it might absorb some of that potent beer as we went.

"Ease up, lad," Brian said as I inhaled a thick bowl of soup and tore at something called a doorstep sandwich. "The potato famine ended years ago." This brought on another round of laughter and more drinks. At least I'd peeled off my blue rain gear by then. If I passed out and hit the deck, I'd seem less like rotting fruit without the blueberry suit.

At some point, between stowing my bike and losing much of the feeling in my cheeks, I reviewed the blind spots in my life, as a young man verging on the edge of drunkenness is apt to do. Everyone has such spots—not obvious shortcomings, but the hidden flaws and conspiring circumstances that duck under the radar, usually until it's too late. Growing up in suburbia, the land of Wonder bread, Campbell's soup, and cul-de-sacs, I harbored a nagging suspicion that my blind spot was somehow tied to a vague feeling of rootlessness. Can anyone really claim a genuine sense of place when the landmarks of their youth are a series of strip malls, golf courses, and 7-Elevens?

A childhood of summer evenings spent floating weightless and womblike in a backyard pool regulated to the temperature of blood . . . for a time I cherished my little monocultural world, taking stock and feeling something close to pleasure in its sameness. The way the automatic sprinklers popped up from hidden turf-builder bunkers each day of each month of each year smacked of utter permanence. A manufactured history, but the only one I'd ever occupied. Mine was a community of Tupperware pioneers making damn certain no one would want for anything they couldn't order from a catalog. I was parochial, insulated, and restless.

It was the writings of a bunch of wayward comrades—London, Conrad, Steinbeck, Twain, and Kerouac—that broke my hermetically sealed (for freshness) world, and all the king's men couldn't put it back together again. For the record, I would have fought them to the death if they'd tried. My outward appearance remained unchanged. I continued to float in the pool, swing in the hammock, pedal the streets, and skate the rails and curbs after class, but a virus had entered my bloodstream. Go get your MBAs and fast tracks—I'll take the road.

Brian asked if I'd buy the gang a shout, and I nodded. God help me, this session was in full swing now.

My first long-distance bicycle adventures were taken out of something close to fear: of growing old before my time, of not seeing and feeling and tasting enough of the world around me before I left it or, worse, grew too jaded to care. I was a middle-class white boy on the road to find out. Sure, I was a cliché. I wanted to say I'd left my zip code and then some. Still, long after the other guys turned in their Eurail passes, stopped writing that Dutch girl they'd met in France, and knocked off the slight British accent, I pedaled on in search of nothing more than moments like this one: a boothful of Irishmen telling lies and teaching me how to pour a proper pint of Guinness.

Act as if you have faith and faith might just find you.

Over the years the road showed me that your place in this world is where you happen to be standing at the moment. Or, in my case, teetering.

Someone stepped into the pub, and I noticed that it was dark outside. When had that happened? I eased back in the booth and tried to focus on the poor sod asleep at the end of the bar. In Ireland the joke goes that Alcoholics Anonymous means a guy who happens to be drinking alone.

"On yere bike," the bartender hollered in the direction of this seemingly comatose fellow. The scuttered gent stirred, found his footing, and wandered for the door.

"That guy's not really going to try to ride a bicycle home, is he?"

This brought such a roar of laughter from the gang in

our booth that you'd have thought I'd just goosed each and every one of them.

The expression had caught my attention several times already during my Irish jaunt, but alcohol and other lively conversation had distracted me from further investigation. I was certainly thrown by it, since none of them appeared to be avid cyclists.

"It's a clever way of telling someone to get off their arse and on with their life," Brian explained. "Out the yard, up your socks, on yere bike."

On yere bike . . . it was the very battle cry I'd been reaching for these many miles in the saddle. My eyes practically filled with grateful tears as I hoisted my glass.

"Gentlemen, on yere bike!" I toasted.

While not moved to my level of emotion, these new-found friends looked plenty amused as our glasses touched. Clearly, I was the only one at the table for whom the phrase carried untold depth and weight. And in the sober and thankfully gray light of an Irish morning the day after, it had only grown more valid as an evocation, rite, fight song, and prayer. Not the sort of thing you'd expect a Tibetan monk to offer up as a mantra, but who would argue with the clarity and simple wisdom of "get off your arse and on with your life"?

Some days I have to coax it from myself as a whisper. Other times I belt it out so loud and strong along lonely stretches of road that quail are flushed from the bush. As long as it rings true, I'm sticking by this as my operating instructions.

On yere bike!

THE ALL-GIRLS
BAGPIPE SQUAD

I've been known to interrupt my regularly scheduled bike tour for a sweet spot in the afternoon sun. Actually, there's a good chance you'll find my rig abandoned most any time of the day if the urge to cloud-gaze and the desire to rest my weary bones overwhelm me. But it's more about the right combination of ground cover, shade, and topography uniting to form what I longingly refer to as the "siesta constellation." You really can't force these little roadside pleasures. I tell rookies to do no more than be open to the concept, allow such opportunities to shine, reveal themselves, and steer them in for a gentle, drowsy landing.

But I don't fall into a complete sleep during my sun-drenched catnaps. Okay, maybe I drift just under the surface, but I'd describe it as a consciously altered state, a hyperreality even, one in which I can still appreciate my surroundings while slipping down a deep well of relaxation, but never so far away that someone could rifle through my stuff unnoticed. At least not until that fateful morning when the all-girls bagpipe squad blew into my dreams. At first I thought it was the Irish countryside whispering its secrets through weathered rock and ancient earth. Then I fancied it a rather textured dream, complete with stunning sound track. But no—I'll be damned if those weren't actual bagpipes carrying rich notes across fields of gold and meadows of green. I finally came around, surfacing to a dry-mouthed stupor of consciousness before stumbling up the rise in the general direction of those powerful pipes.

Cynics say that love at first sight is the disease of hopeless romantics and the hope of greedy greeting-card companies romancing your wallet, but when my eyes locked upon a dozen or so winsome young women—maybe first-year college students—blowing into bagpipes beside a bus, it felt as if Cupid had skewered me with every arrow in his quiver. After that he flew down for some close-in work, twisting the shafts, then breaking them off inside me for good measure.

Sweet weeping Jesus, I have to say that these women were sirens of mythological proportions. Their outfits, traditional billowing white blouses and short dark skirts with knee-high socks, took my mind straight through to all that pent-up Catholic-school sexual repression as a fashion statement. They played some more, and I longed to wreck myself on their nubile shores.

First, though, I had to fix my biker hair—a herculean task, since a bike helmet never met a hairstyle it couldn't wreck. I spat into my hands and matted the unruly mess down as much as possible. I had no mirror to confirm my handiwork, but by my guess, it was as good as it was going to get. As I plucked off some stray remnants of breakfast stuck to my jersey and drew a deep, centering breath in anticipation of marching myself down the hill, I caught the piercing whine of truck brakes coming to a stop alongside my bike, which anyone might reasonably have mistaken for abandoned. I stood frozen for a long, pained moment, the all-girls bagpipe squad on one side and on the other a bewildered gent searching around the Irish countryside for the owner of a ditched bicycle.

"Don't go anywhere, my honey-sweet sirens." I either whispered this aloud or thought it with such force that it broke clear of my cranium. What I do know for sure is that I charged down the hill so fast and excitedly after my bicycle that the truck driver might have taken my approach for a very low-budget battle scene from the film *Braveheart,* an outtake featuring an army of one: "They will never take our freedom! Or at the very least our bicycles."

He stepped back, no doubt eyeing me for any visible weapons and clear signs of mental instability.

"I wasn't going to pinch it, you see," he declared once I was in earshot. "Just making certain you hadn't managed a spill and needed assistance."

"And I'm much in your debt." Nearly breathless, I extended a smile and a bike-gloved mitt in his direction. It's incredibly bad form in Ireland to be abrupt with people— anywhere, really, but especially in Ireland, where you must sway and bend to the laconic, neighborly way that folks outside the big city meander through conversations. As a rule, this is my favorite part of travel, the holy grail in fact: to chat about nothing in particular and feel completely in the present.

But that morning it was like having my teeth pulled. As he spoke I could no longer detect the precious pipers' plaintive wails, and I was hard pressed to concentrate on anything the friendly gent was talking about. He used a lot of wide, arcing hand gestures, I remember that much. It's a wonder he didn't ask me what I'd been smoking. With every slow nod, smile, and two-, three-, or four-part question from the truck driver, my gifted girls were making their exodus to points unknown.

"Now, do you sleep directly on the ground or . . ." He paused. "Is there a tent tucked away in those . . . what do you call those nifty bags?" Longer pause. "They look right useful."

After I'd fended off multiple offers of a lift anywhere in the county and endured the laborious process of watching this kindly Samaritan ponder over the writing of his address on the back of an old receipt like it was the signing of the Magna Carta, he added, "You'll stop by and have a hot meal with us now, right?" I told him to count on it and, like an indentured servant, was finally cut loose, free at last to sprint up the hill.

The squad, of course, had set sail, but worse still, they'd managed to clear the horizon. I tried to remember which way the nose of the bus had been pointed, but my brain had paid far more attention to the comely lassies blowing the bags. In a moment of desperation I glanced back to see if my truck driver was still hanging around. Certainly I could press him into service. Damn. He was a leisurely talker but a zippy leadfoot. It was not a question of whether I would pursue the all-girls bagpipe squad, but how much of Ireland I would have to cover to find them. I hauled my bike over the hill and headed south for no other reason than I had to start somewhere. It had been a light blue bus . . . or was that the color of the emblems on their blouses? A converted school bus deal, maybe? A top-notch detective conducting an airtight dragnet, I was not.

The shopkeeper smiled, nodding with what appeared to be recognition. A break in the case. "If it's bagpipes you're interested in, then you must talk to the Major."

Before I could protest, she was ringing up the retired gentleman, who, as it happened, didn't have anything more pressing at hand and said he'd come right over. I thought seriously about excusing myself to the bathroom and fleeing the town limits in advance of the Major's assault, but that was just the ferocious love bite of the all-girls bagpipe squad talking. I knew I was stuck.

"A Yank reporter touring the country, then, doing a piece on our traditions. Splendid. We don't get nearly enough interest in the pipes on that side of the pond."

I'd invented my cover on the spot: a profile piece for a leisure magazine. It sounded better than explaining to this rather proper-looking man that I'd just been smitten by a busload of pipe-playing beauties whom I now intended to stalk by bicycle around the length and breadth of his fine country.

The Major came prepared. He had several sets of pipes in tow, and another sticking out of his mouth—strictly for tobacco consumption. Sitting with me on a bench across from the shop, the Major revealed that he'd done a bit of bicycle riding while in the service. "I'd keep the pedal and crank equipment handy and when we touched down in country, if it wasn't too hostile or loaded with land mines, I'd have a ride around. Do I envy you, lad." He took a puff on his unlit pipe. "I've always said it's something of a poetic approach to seeing the world."

The Major was so earnest about his pipe passion, and no minor historian on the subject, that I had to lock the boisterous girls away inside my head for a spell and dig around the depths of my rear panniers until I came up with a reporter's pad. I started taking notes for a phantom article on Irish traditions. I lost significant ground in the hunt for the bagpiping beauties, the better part of that afternoon, but gained knowledge and insight into the Scottish Highland bagpipe and its oboelike relative, the Irish uilleann pipe.

Being an absolute beginner on the subject, I thought that one make, model, and size of bagpipe fit all. When I exposed my ignorance to the Major he tried to control his disappointment behind a flurry of pipe smoking, but I might as well have boxed his ears for the obvious pain I'd inflicted.

It turns out the Scottish Highland bagpipe is the first team of pipes—it was created in the 1500s in the mountainous, Gaelic-speaking regions of the Highlands and western islands of Scotland. You play it by blowing on a reed into a chanter. The melody comes from a fixed scale of nine notes. Those other big, upright pipes are called drones. They play a single constant bass/treble tone. It's all connected to a bag held under your arm that fills with air. I told the Major it reminded me of someone putting a massive spider into a headlock.

"You have quite the imagination."

If he only knew what my imagination was doing with the all-girls bagpipe squad.

Irish uilleann pipes have been called the most elaborate bagpipe in the world. It's as if a roomful of college engineering students searched for an already complicated musical device and adopted it as their senior project. Those babies hit the market in Ireland around the 1700s. The Major explained that the word *uilleann* (pronounced "ILL-en") comes from the Irish for "elbow." Folks also call it the union pipe or the organ pipe.

"You don't blow it with your mouth, but inflate it using bellows. Folks like its two-octave range and the fact that you can sing while playing," the Major said. "Personally, I don't feel singing is necessary when you have pipes. Have you ever tried listening for the triangle player over a full symphony orchestra?"

I sat back. My girls had definitely been blowing into traditional pipes. "Maybe they're a Scottish group touring Ireland?"

"Who?"

It was time to come clean with the Major. I just wasn't focusing on the interview enough to bluff anymore. He took it well. I promised to use my notes in a journalistic fashion at some point, but he waved me off. It appeared the Major had a soft spot in his heart for a woman who could play the pipes.

"Their dress doesn't sound traditional, but then this wasn't a performance. Simple practicing by the side of the road, you say? I can give you the addresses of piping clubs from Donegal to Galway, but it's likely a needle in a haystack. Best to consider yourself lucky, you getting to enjoy such a spontaneous show, such as it were." The Major seemed to be catching a touch of my fever.

He puffed and pondered in response to my query. No, "My wife does not play. . . . Now, tell me again how they held their notes. Did some of them stand in a circle or do any marching? Was there a drummer?"

I left the Major to his daydreams, but only after he made me promise I'd call when I solved the mystery.

If the squad existed outside my memory, it was fast and elusive. Rumored sightings came and went as quickly as the appearance of sunshine on the Eastern coast. I picked up a scent from a club member in Limerick only to be introduced to a pair of grammar-school sisters making joyfully horrendous noises into pint-sized pipes. It was the sound I imagined livestock produced when being tortured. I'll say this, though—their matching outfits had stage appeal in a *Soul Train*–meets–*Star Search* kind of way.

I found myself standing in fields, parks, and other vast spaces—anywhere far from laws governing noise ordinances—wading through one piping club's practice session after another. Make no mistake, many of these players were quite good, but like the violin and the starter drum set, bagpipes should come with their own soundproof room until the player reaches a certain skill level.

It was only a matter of time before my hosts would hook me up to one of the Highland varieties and ask me to blow into the reed for all I was worth. While this provided me with an appreciation for the effort and musicianship involved (it's not how hard you blow but the technique), it did not help me to block out the aerial bombardment of novice players at work. One bad piper in a group can turn a majestic melody into a traffic jam. There's a fine line between a masterfully handled dirge and the siren blasts set up around nuclear power plants or those piercing tests for the emergency broadcasting system.

In all my travels, I've never met a cyclist who toured with bagpipes aboard. It's not the same as a harmonica or penny whistle. They just don't pack well, and I suspect one would have a helluva time landing invites into people's homes, not to mention the potential for alienating campground pals. Maybe it's just human nature to restrict behavior to one semifreakish hobby at a time. And trust me—riding thousands of miles on a bike is considered freakish by many folks. But like cyclists, the bagpiping community is a self-aware subculture. Most know that others find them slightly odd and don't really understand why they choose to do what they do. This endeared me to them more and allowed my eardrums to endure what sometimes amounted to musical torture.

And just as when the wind is at the perfect angle to a cyclist's back, the pedal cadence finds a sweet spot, and you shimmer along as if you've taken flight, the magic of a perfectly pitched song blown on the pipes helps people transcend their worries and wants. A soulful piper at a funeral or a marching contingent blowing loud and proud offers a glimpse behind life's curtain.

From large men sweating their way through practice sessions in church basements, reeking of cigarettes and beer, to a mother-daughter team whose tunes veered from traditional piping into a punk-polka hybrid, probably ten years ahead of its time (you'll see it on MTV one of these days, mark my words), I scared up damn near every piper in Ireland, except for my all-girls bagpipe squad.

By the time I'd wheeled it back to Dublin I'd long since called off the hunt. During another siesta in a park, this time with my eyes wide open, I noticed a guy practicing on a penny canter. People use these so they don't disturb birds and set off car alarms in a five-mile radius. I introduced myself for no other reason than I wanted to talk some smack about the bagpipe and come off as an educated American on the subject. We chatted for a while, and I was glad I'd struck up a conversation. My friend was a boisterous Brit hitchhiking around the country. Depleted finances were finally forcing him back home.

"You been playing long?" I asked.

"Funny story. I was staying the night at this church in County Cork. The rain was lashing me something wicked before they took pity on me. Come the morning service, a group of women bagpipers played after communion. They were brilliant and not hard on the eyes, mind you. I'd call it the first religious experience I've ever achieved inside a church. The whole affair stuck with me, so much so that I bought this little penny canter a few weeks ago. I'm going to get some proper lessons back home when I can cobble together a few quid."

I wanted to launch into an interrogation like he was a high-profile murder suspect. *Were they traveling in a blue bus? How many of them were there? Names? Home phone numbers? Do you know where they are now?*

But I was flying out of Ireland on the morning plane. It was enough to have confirmation that the all-girls bagpipe squad was alive, well, and part of waking reality. It was enough to know they were crisscrossing Europe and beyond, breaking hearts and sending men on vision quests and walkabouts with each performance.

"It must have been a helluva show," I said.

"You can't even imagine," he replied.

I smiled. Oh, yes, I could, and I would for years to come.

MR. ICE CREAM MAN

What powers the machine?
Desire, desire, desire.
—BLIND TOM

Can someone who didn't have a permanent address for years at a time consider himself—in good conscience, mind you—a creature of habit? I'm not sure. All the same, set me down in one spot for a few days and I'll wear ruts in the road pedaling to my favorite haunts and shopping at the nearest family-owned market, where right off they're calling me by name.

It's a rhythm that never takes long to establish. I always manage to locate a choice piece of overlooked real estate along a skyline trail or canyon road. A refuge to rest the bones and catch the sunset. And let's not forget a lively pub or paddock bar where the shadows and generous flow of ale help to take years off my brow and those around me. Most people just look a little better when the sun goes down. That's why they named it happy hour.

It happened in Aruba, again in Perth, and boy, did I ever slip into a nice routine in Puerto Vallarta. Not so much in Detroit, but I was schooled by the locals that no one should get too comfortable in that town. The Motor City aside, be it County Clare, Ireland, or Alice Springs, Australia, when I hang my helmet and call someplace my temporary home, it's time to mark the territory, create a familiar circuit and make it my own. Mind you, I'm not some sort of type-A, Walkman-wearing, Palm Pilot–punching control freak. Rather, I tend to organically slip into a groove, a routine of sorts, if given even a little time and space. Maybe it's tied to some deep-seated need to feel more secure within a nomadic existence. Whatever the psychosocial ramifications are (and such things are better left to folks who didn't spend their college psych courses mentally cataloging and recataloging a very extensive music collection), the routine nearly always includes a daily bike ride. One of the most memorable patches of this kind of riding was in Mexico.

Circumstances found me and the bike hunkered down on a rather pleasant side of La Paz. I was calling the beachfront portion of Baja's seaside capital home for a few days. Friends were to rendezvous with me for a sea kayaking adventure, but until they made their grand entrance, I was forced to endure ice-cold beer at dirt-cheap prices, a living hell if there ever was one.

An actual palm tree grew right there inside the private patio of our suite at La Posada de Engelbert—yes, the one and only Engelbert Humperdinck, he of the classy floor show, stylish toe tapping, and ballad crooning. The man had purchased this place during the sixties and more than likely forgotten about it except during tax season. This could have been the reason no one had received the green light yet to wreck the hotel's charm with a remodel. Whatever the situation was surrounding La Posada de Engelbert, it exuded some serious kitsch. Bobby Darin tunes played over the pool speakers, and the entire lounge appeared to have been airlifted directly from a *Hawaii Five-O* set. On this afternoon, obscene amounts of chips and guacamole arrived next to my patio chair like clockwork. I kept thinking,

Good gordita, *I have to find a bike ride, stat . . . anything to stave off the plaque from completely gumming my arteries before sunset.* Darin's buoyant rendition of "Beyond the Sea" almost sucked me back into the depths of the patio furniture for good, but I reached deep inside myself, clipped into the pedals, and spun through thick sand . . . straight on to daylight.

Back, you devil avocado, back.

I'd worked up a decent sweat when the Mexican kids caught me. They were riding relic Huffys, one-speed banana-seat clunkers, and Schwinn speedsters (an oxymoron if there ever was one). I'm speaking of those proper rigs with upright "gentleman" handlebars, a favorite among Ivy League freshmen on their way to glee club practice.

A gang of five or six of these kids hung close to my wheel only to drop off down a side street many dusty blocks later. I blamed the chips and guacamole for my condition that day and didn't give my lackluster pace another thought. To say it worried me when a few of these boys pedaled ahead on day two would be accurate, but when the entire pack stayed with me for a good half-mile sprint on day three, talking cheerfully in Spanish and packing too much relaxed energy, I started to question my own abilities on a bicycle. For the record, when I use the term *kids,* it's not middle-aged-man-speak. I'm not referring to college-age bucks but actual children—eleven or twelve years old at most. The rest of the week the same group of pedal pushers would blitz out from a side street, stay on my tail for a number of blocks, then bank through an intersection and disappear into the heat.

Were they taunting me without saying a word? *Watch us*

race this big American retard on his expensive rig just for the sport of it. *Go USA! Go USA!*

If this wasn't the case, I asked myself, then where the hell were they going in such a hurry? I'm talking about full-out sprints on crapola bicycles for healthy distances.

The day before my own pals arrived for our kayak trip, I just had to know what was what. When the kids banked through the intersection, this time I banked with them. For several more blocks we kept up a torturous pace. The kids, in their ratty sneakers, homemade tank tops, and cutoff blue jeans, peered back over their shoulders, all nods and smiles when they saw that I was now in hot pursuit. And that's when I heard it. The jingle of happy bells, growing stronger with each passing street. *I'm your Mr. Ice Cream Man, stop me when I'm passing by.*

All this time the pack had been chasing the good stuff: bomb pops, chewy clusters, and Eskimo Pies. I braked hard beside the truck, laughing like a *turista* too long in the sun. As the kids grabbed for their treats and leaned back in their saddles, slurping and chomping with abandon, I caught a damn strong vibe. It was the vibe of someone I hadn't been this close to since summer vacations with my own bike-riding brothers in arms. Right there, bathing in the warm embrace between memory and dream, was my former self: a twelve-year-old sitting loose and casual on a blue Schwinn Sting Ray like it was yesterday afternoon. How I wanted to crawl back inside that reckless, supple skin and live there again, for even a moment.

Since that wasn't possible, I bought an oversized ice cream sandwich—the Neapolitan kind, to properly honor my former self and the many miles now between us.

Here I'd thought I was the main attraction for these Mexican grade-schoolers, but the powers of the universe and the pure desires of kids in every culture proved me insignificant once again. They were speaking a different language than my childhood gang ever did, and about two decades separated us from them, but other than that it was a time machine—I was back on the Sting Ray and back on the old block.

When I really stop and think it through, my own pint-size posse north of the border, the one I glided with down back streets and around cul-de-sacs on those long summer days, was all about routines, too. Most mornings we'd spend trolling the unmowed edges of the highway for empty pop bottles, or we'd coast our bikes along the storm runoff culverts, miles of concrete ravines ripe with treasures. People during that time disregarded the advice of that seventies environmental icon Woodsy Owl and his chirpy slogan "Give a Hoot, Don't Pollute" and tossed redeemable income labeled Pepsi, Busch, and Budweiser out of their car windows and into our wallets.

Once our packs were heavy with cans and bottles, we'd make our way over to an enigmatically named convenience store called Little General and cash out our winnings like high rollers leaving Vegas. The Little General logo staring down at us appeared litigiously similar to that of the cartoon character Yosemite Sam, only with Elvis-length sideburns bordering on mutton chops and more of a Napoleonic glare than Pancho Villa's fury. No one liked the store much, but it was the best place on earth to cash bottles. The 7-Eleven got our business, but the clerks at the Little General just let us pour the bottles and cans into that shopping cart in the corner and make up an inflated number that sounded mildly reasonable. They hated working at Little General and showed it by paying us too much for our efforts. It was our good fortune that the Yosemite Sam knock-off didn't instill much loyalty in his employees.

If there wasn't anything interesting playing at the dollar matinee or anything we could talk our way into without adult supervision, we'd roll by the abandoned warehouse district and throw bricks, sticks, metal, or rocks through any windows that weren't completely broken yet. The mall, while air-conditioned, always grew boring about a week into vacation, so we'd race over to Howard food market to harass the pudgy owner by ordering one Cuban sandwich for five guys. We'd pass it around like a joint until it and the Mountain Dew were gone, or the normally affable owner, a Cuban guy, chased us off his curb with a hose full of hot water and a wire push broom.

The gloves and bats aboard our bikes were for playground-league baseball three days a week. We rounded out the incendiary part of the afternoon with a daily stop at the Jewish community center for swimming, foosball, pool, and Ping-Pong. The fact that only one of us was Jewish and no one was an actual member didn't break our stride. The first week of the summer we commandeered the names of kids like Morty Finestein and Abel Segal, who were off making something of their futures at places like math camp and the Brandeis Institute. Brash charm and easy confidence ruled the day. Pretty soon everyone knew us, and we stopped having to sign in under any name at all. The highlight of each summer came when we'd be banned from the game room for a week because we'd been caught sharking some of the real members out of snack money.

"Next time this happens we're calling your parents," the director, who doubled as the swim coach, announced, not unkindly. "And damn it," he said, "you boys are what makes this place a joy, so let's not have to place those calls."

Yes, let's not. It would have only confused and befuddled the parental units. I can hear it now: "Honey, the boys have gotten into some sort of trouble while doing community service for Jewish people."

But my favorite part of any summer day was buying Nehi sodas and bags of Funyuns, or more often a jumbo-size watermelon. We'd shoot bottle caps for distance to see who had to carry the beast of a melon on the back of his bike. When we reached the seawall one of us would demonstrate the traditional hobo carving method—drop the oversized fruit against a curb—and pass out various odd-shaped pieces. No one argued the presentation or the division of melon. We just took our seats along the still-warm pavement, munched the sweet pulp, spit seeds into the water, watched a killer light show on the horizon, and talked about stuff that mattered to us.

Between easy chatter dominated by girls, music, and movies, I'd mention on occasion that wouldn't it be cool to ride away on our bikes, all of us, just go and go . . . until we might even find ourselves back in the same spot a year or two later.

This was sunset talk that everyone agreed to with unbridled enthusiasm and forgot about in the next breath. Still, I want to believe that my old gang, gone, scattered to the winds (or some still even hunkered down in our old zip code, for all I know), would have gotten a kick out of my chase to catch the Mexican kids as they pedaled after the simple pleasures of the ice cream man. Or at the very least they'd have related, recognizing the clean sweat and unforced laughter as that of a distant, shimmering summer.

Their summer. Our summer. *The* summer.

Maybe that's why my tours by bike always begin and end solo, but during most of the miles between I happily share lanes, drafts, dinners, and tent sites with other spoke-singing, kindred souls—refugees from their own childhood posses who, like me, actually followed up the crazy idea of going too far on a bicycle.

THE CANTALOUPES
OF WRATH

If I have an Achilles' heel, it would have to be cantaloupe. More than nourishment, time and again that sweet melon has restored my faith in a higher force, for the simple reason that nothing so delicious could be produced without some sort of divine intervention.

Certainly not much to hang a theological dissertation on, but it works for me. Think about it: For years, roving missionaries and Bible-toting doorbell ringers could have saved time and energy and reduced the risk of humiliation—not to mention saved on printing costs—by delivering boxes of ripe cantaloupe with a note that reads

THERE IS A GOD. ENJOY MY MELONS.

Needless to say, with this sort of mind-set, if I'm offered anything from full crates to bite-size slices of that orange ambrosia, there's no turning back.

Pedaling one sweltering afternoon along a riverside back road near the Gray Ranch in northern Mexico, I spied a field of melons fat and ripe in the midmorning sun. Like a Muslim at prayer hour, I stopped and got down on my knees to pay silent tribute. That's when a beater truck—a classic southwest farmer's vehicle—that was parked side-ways next to the field caught my eye. Its driver, a pear-shaped fellow with graying stubble and a sweat-stained cowboy hat, nodded from a threadbare lawn chair.

"Nice crop," I praised with too much enthusiasm.

He might have grinned. We made eye contact.

I couldn't help myself. "You mind if I pick a 'loupe or two on the house? I've been pedaling this road awhile."

Lawn Chair Man shrugged. In English he said, "Pick as many as you like."

It was as if security had left Vegas.

I went to work, even going so far as to take out my knife and munch on some slices right there in the field. I loaded my bike jersey pockets to overflowing. As the number of melons I'd managed to stuff in my panniers seemed fairly outrageous, I kept looking back at him for an indication that I'd stepped over the line.

He yawned and stretched a little, like a big cat in the sun. I took this to mean there must be a good profit margin in 'loupes. It seemed like a fine time to inquire as to the corn in the next acreage, but I was interrupted by a shiny half-ton pickup that roared, skidded, and careened to a gravity-defying stop a few feet from my bike, dust flying everywhere. The driver looked sufficiently pissed.

"What the hell are you doing with my cantaloupes?" he exploded with as he snatched a melon out of my hand.

I pointed at Lawn Chair Man. "This guy said it was fine."

Angry Farmer and I waited there for a long, tense moment while Lawn Chair Man lumbered to his feet, scratched his chest a few times, then spoke. "Why should I mind? My truck ran out of gas right about here and I was waiting for someone to let me hop a ride to town."

Closing my eyes, I flashed to Peter Sellers in that Pink Panther movie:

SELLERS: "Does your dog bite?"
CLERK: "No."
Sellers gets bitten.
SELLERS: "I thought you said your dog didn't bite."
CLERK: "That's not my dog."

Those movies still make me wet my pants with laughter.

I looked over at the melons, and though I was probably in for a beating if not jail time, the sight of them made me feel better. No matter what life throws at you, it's comforting to have at least one precious thing to believe in.

Fortunately, the real cantaloupe farmer had something of a sense of humor. After I told him the Peter Sellers bit, I was even allowed to keep a number of those plump 'loupes. In what should not have been mistaken as a sign of maturity, I pedaled away without asking about the corn.

DUMPSTER DIVING
WITH SAMMY D.

It's amazing what a subscription to *Smithsonian* can do for the appearance of one's IQ, if not the actual number. For instance, I can say with conviction that if you drop two Ping-Pong balls into the ocean at the very same place and time, one may wash up in Nantucket and the other is just as likely to end its journey stuck to the edge of an iceberg in Antarctic waters. Scientists have spent years and millions of grant dollars determining that the ocean makes its own rules.

Don't ask me why, but I sleep better knowing we have so little control over two-thirds of the earth's surface.

Each time I load up my trusty bike and spin away from the front door, I feel an affinity with those balls drifting through unknowing currents. I'm not as round as one—not yet, anyway—and I certainly don't bounce worth a damn, as evidenced during a recent tumble from my bike, and the last time I checked, I didn't have the Spalding logo tattooed across my arse, but like those balls, once I roll away on two wheels, I could end up just about anywhere. Thinking of the possibilities at the beginning of any bike trip makes me giddy, covered in goose bumps, revived, and flush with a certain nervous energy. It's the same flutter and snap that I knew as a kid waiting next in line for the roller coaster or standing in the on-deck circle confidently swinging a heavy baseball bat while the big game hung in the balance. Rolling anywhere, on or off the map, always makes me tense up like first love.

It doesn't matter one bit whether I'm sweating the pedals over Kicking Horse Pass in Canada just ahead of a late-spring snowstorm or feeling my vision blur as I limp my bicycle into Reed, Australia, just as long as it isn't some spot on the map I'd recognize in bad lighting or inclement weather. Home Sweet Home makes a comfortable motto to cross-stitch onto a quilt while trapped indoors for the duration of a long winter, but I like this one better: Papa Was a Rolling Stone.

To my own credit or folly, I let momentum lead the way. I like to think of the world as a grab bag, one that I rarely peek inside before the party gets rolling. It could be hauling my bike into a dugout canoe in hopes of successfully crossing a rain-swollen river in Peru or pushing my cumbersome rig up the side of some mountain that a distracted cartographer omitted on the map. High tides, low bridges, or renegade camping spots . . . Maybe I'm just too lazy to bother with details like planning. Had I kept to a rigid schedule, I never would have slept in an Irish castle or played Ping-Pong with a Cuban prodigy in Venezuela. Then again, scheduling certainly might have kept me from freezing my butt off in Alaska and that bowel-releasing encounter with a grizzly who just wanted to dance. I could have done without those.

Some people, especially high-tech buddies I've discussed the topic with, find my approach to travel maddening—terrifying, actually, on the same level as scoring below a

300 on the math portion of their SATs. Not to mention they categorize it as a woefully inefficient way to manage one's time. What goes right over their heads is that real adventure should thumb its nose at time *and* management.

But I'm not alone in this way of thinking.

I once spied this chap in the Baltimore airport, weighed down with a backpack and anchored in front of a bank of departure screens, eyes closed, running his finger lightly over random locales like a blind man reading Braille. When that roulette ball of a digit finally came to rest, his eyes snapped open—we had a winner. He gave the slightest twitch of a nod, grabbed up his bag, and headed for the ticket counter. Now that's how it's done, sports fans.

Yes, this wayward gentleman is to be considered the Antichrist by travel agents and looked upon as a leper by guidebook companies, but on the border between chaos and tourism, he towers mightily over all he surveys, at least in my eyes. His patented technique is how I ended up a hairsbreadth away from Central America. Actually, I arrived there after a frightfully circuitous meander through the dusty bowels of Copper Canyon, Mexico, but the spirit of my plans was much the same—spin around inside my head until I was emotionally dizzy, close my eyes when it all became too much to clarify using the known senses alone, draw myself inward, and press hard enough to alchemize into a human magnet. Then shake vigorously and allow this new form of life I've morphed into to pull me in the direction of something—call it adventure, call it time out of mind, but understand it need not be big and flashy, just unplanned and off the books. Presto—life spits you out in a distant land. This time around it was Acapulco.

Without my lack of guiding principles I never would have washed up onto Sammy D., who was Dumpster-diving the better bins at resort hotels in this sun-drenched paradise.

Some people strap on scuba gear and explore reefs and sunken ships, while others with even more backbone dive the tight spaces of underwater caves, but Sammy D. and his dog, Quantum Leap, navigated the pungent world of refuse. I would soon discover what it meant to believe with all of one's heart and eco-friendly soul that Dumpster diving can save the world.

Sammy D. gave me quite a start. I was leaning against the back wall of a resort hotel, trying to figure out where my listening skills had gone astray. This certainly wasn't the $5-a-night youth hostel on the beach I'd been assured I'd find at these coordinates. A sweet little border collie leashed to some metal fencing barked at me while I scanned the area for someone I could bother about new directions. Then the lid of the Dumpster sprang open with such force that I fully expected a mammoth creature from the underworld to rise out of the bin, swallow me whole, bellow with satisfaction, and retreat back into the darkness.

Instead, a sun-baked gentleman, maybe pushing fifty, poked out his head.

"Good dog," he whispered. If not for the fact that he was inside a Dumpster, this man resembled many of the yacht club parents I knew from hanging out on my pal Clark Mercer's boat during summer vacation. Wearing deck shoes, a spotless polo shirt, Dockers, and an expensive-looking watch, the man hoisted himself with the agility of a teenager out of the bin, executing a fluid dismount that would have impressed all but the Russian judges.

For a brief moment I thought maybe he was an American working for the hotel who'd been asked to search for the gold cuff links some wealthy guest tossed by mistake. But Sammy D. smiled politely in my direction, gathered up a collection of treasures that he'd stacked on top of the lid, unhitched his dog, and wandered behind the Dumpster for a moment. When he emerged, the theme song to TV's *Sanford and Son* jumped into my head. Sammy D.'s oversized trike was crammed with goods. I observed a framed painting, two VCRs, stacks of magazines, some CDs, and bags of fresh fruit.

There was a metal basket in front. His dog leapt into it without prompting. I knew I had to pedal after Sammy D. The youth hostel was just gonna be loaded with people like me, anyway.

Sammy explained that the majority of stuff on his bike had been gathered that day. He was on his way to sell some of it to vendors at the *mercados* and he'd take some of it home, but not before dropping certain needed items and the surplus food at charity centers that would get it into deserving hands and mouths.

At one of the stops I caught our reflections in a mirrored window and had to laugh. To anyone sizing up the two of us, I more closely resembled a Dumpster diver than Sammy D.

Everyone had a wave and a handshake for Sammy D., an extra minute or two for this treasure hunter of trash. He was such a soft-spoken gem of a man, the spitting image of Mr. Rogers, had he chosen recycling over children's television as a career.

I noticed that one item never left Sammy D.'s rig. It was

a retractable pole. He called it his treasure grabber. It was built to stab, poke, hold, and pick up anything. There was a place to attach a magnet on the end.

"You caught me inside the bin today. That's rare. Most of the time I don't have to leave my feet." He patted his retractable pole, extending it into the locked position like a light saber. "I fished out a Skil saw with my grabber once, and loose pesos don't stand a chance against this master magnet."

I was in the presence of a black belt in the not-so-ancient art of Dumpster diving.

"You make this pole yourself?"

"Nah, this I ordered out of a catalog and tweaked it with a few improvements."

It turned out to be one of the only items he'd ever bought retail. Sammy D. walked me through the rest of his gear. It included trash bags, duct tape, diaper wipes for cleaning up, and a fold-out stepladder.

"Sometimes you need a few extra feet of height to angle for the grab, and I've learned that standing on the side of a Dumpster can be dangerous," explained Sammy D.

The food he scored from the resort Dumpsters verged on gourmet. That day the needy whom Sammy D. shared with would be eating fresh croissants, drinking from nearly full containers of orange juice, and buttering up poppy-seed bagels. Sammy's trike came complete with a good-sized cooler (found near a Dumpster at the beach), where he stored perishable foods, drink containers, and the like.

"You know, my trike was a throwaway. It's mind-boggling how much we toss out." Sammy had been diving for a decade, yet his amazement at the banality of excess and devaluation of goods in a disposable society had not waned. I would learn that North America trashes about 100 billion pounds of perfectly good stuff each year. And Sammy's biggest regret? That he was only one guy with a trike and a grabber tool.

"I worked for one of the big three insurance companies. Every day in that place felt more and more like being waist deep in garbage, let me tell you." We were now back at his house, a simple bungalow decked out with top-drawer goods—some really awesome items, most of which he'd rescued from the bins, gathered on the incoming tide, or found with his trusty metal detector. A quick survey revealed boxes of greeting cards, appliances of every stripe, musical instruments, and on and on. Surprisingly, it didn't have a cluttered, pack-rat feel. He wasn't a hoarder. Sammy gave away all that he didn't absolutely need. When he wasn't working the Dumpsters, Sammy D. was working on his tan while listening through headphones for buried treasure. He reminded me of one of those antiheroes at the end of a heist movie, the guys who get away clean to have their day under the warm glow of a Mexican sun.

"People suspect that they're always just a day or two away from where they want to be. With me, I couldn't stand to look out at the sun from behind double plate glass anymore."

Sammy passed a nearly full bag of Marriott's best pistachio nuts my way. Remarkably fresh and tasty.

"I can't describe what it was that finally pushed me out the door. I do remember thinking, 'Sammy, you're a few cards shy of a deck—you don't have the money to retire unless you plan to drop dead on the third Wednesday around three P.M. following your official retirement party.' But as I thought about it some more, really looked at it, what was I protecting? I'd been too busy working to start a family, to start much of anything. I didn't even have a cat, so I decided to walk away and just see what would happen."

What happened was that Sammy D. had more than enough after he taught himself to capture the excesses of a careless, mass-produced world. "When you take a good look around, you realize that most of us think, 'Hell, just throw it out, 'cause hey, we'll always be able to make more.' "

We talked deep into the night. It was very enlightening. If not for that chat I wouldn't know, for instance, that retail stores have specific times of the week or month when the best stuff is tossed in the Dumpster, condo bins at the end of high season are like Christmas day to a Dumpster diver, and the average pack rat only spends about ten dollars a month on food. We walked down to the beach, where Sammy D. was always supplying the net jockeys with new Wilsons and Spaldings. They called him Pops even though he was in better shape than some of them.

"Look for these colored pieces of glass," Sammy D. instructed, showing me a green chunk of bottle smoothed by the constant pounding of surf and sand.

We were walking the water's edge. "The yellow and purple shards are the best," he explained. "That's what I really need most." Sammy was nearly finished with the construction of a wedding arch and wanted a bit more smoothed glass for the mosaic patterns at the top. Seems Sammy was an artist as well as king of the Dumpster divers. He'd been commissioned to create a piece by a middle-class family with some real standing in the community.

"They spotted one of my archways at this other wedding, one I made for a dirt-poor couple, friends of mine I wanted to help. The bride and groom exchanged their vows in the square across from their church because they didn't have any money to pay for a proper service."

When the middle-class family asked Sammy how much one of his creations would cost, he explained it wasn't a matter of money, but about meeting the pair who were to be married. He needed to spend time with them so he could decide what should go into the arch. When pressed, he added that the other couple's groom had paid in full for the creation by helping Sammy D. Dumpster-dive a few mornings a week, long before he ever asked for an arch. In fact, the arch had been Sammy D.'s idea.

"The dad gave me an obscene wad of money just so I'd stop talking about Dumpsters. But the kids getting married are all right. I'm happy to do it for them."

Later, helping Sammy D. steady the new arch while he attached a few glass-shard-laden tiles, I noticed flecks of green paper twisted into the yellow crepe-paper flowers that rimmed the outsides of his work.

"Are these marigolds made out of . . . money?"

Sammy D. flashed a wicked little grin. "I had to do something with Papa's wad. This has to be a labor of love or it won't come out right."

That evening as I stood under Sammy's arch, a cooling breeze off the water arrived like a promise. Sammy was having a drink from some vintage scotch he'd rescued away from a Dumpster while on winter holiday in San Marces. I counted stars through intricate latticework and wondered what such an installation could fetch in the finer galleries of

Los Angeles or New York. The insurance world's loss, the art world's gain. Then again, what would be the point of commercializing such singular beauty? You can't just sell one-of-a-kind creations born of the dumps and nurtured along the shores of Mexico. Or you could, but something would get lost in the process. I suspected it would be Sammy D.

He wandered out of the house and over to his arch, gently touching a spot and adjusting a flower until he was satisfied. Here was a late bloomer who had finally started something worth seeing through. I should be so lucky.

"Will you take me diving tomorrow, Sammy?"

He handed me a glass of scotch. "I thought you'd never ask."

ALWAYS LOOK TO THE LEFT
OF YOUR RIGHT-HAND MAN

Just after finding my way clear of the jungles, I was flanked by the fastest pair of Mormons on two wheels. A day of hard riding had me tantalizingly close to the bathwater-warm coastal surf of southern Mexico. This piece of knowledge helped slightly improve my average cruising speed. Like a faithful old riding horse that smells the barn near the end of a long day, I actually had something of a kick in the legs—a gear-aided gallop, even—when those Mormon brothers barreled down on me.

My plan to that point was to locate a ramshackle oasis, a brightly colored bar or dirt-floor dive where one could drink *cerveza* without restraint. There I would tell some slightly inflated renderings of my adventures to anyone speaking better than broken English. Even a booth of new-found amigos or a bar stool with one friendly *compadre* who couldn't comprehend three words of it but smiled pleasantly and nodded with confidence at my bravado-laced yammering—this would do fine.

But when those boys dressed in their crisp black-and-white Sunday best glided hard and fast to within inches of my rear wheel . . . all bets were off.

Sharp and shockingly fresh for that late in the day, this

pair resembled a couple of God-fearing Blues Brothers swooping down from a side road on some urgent mission to points and states of mind unknown. Not having to carry much gear gave them an advantage, but I pedaled the good fight all the same. Shimmering waters along the coast offered something beyond resplendent beauty and a measure of comfort when my lungs felt ready to cave in. I hummed "Onward Christian Soldiers," and the hint of a tailwind on the final push to the beach didn't hurt my chances either.

I'm not sure why I had to keep up. It could have been the natural laws of testosterone, congealing with a certain righteous indignation, that dictated that men in flare-legged slacks purchased on sale at JC Penney should not best a guy in proper cycling Lycra.

"Is everyone from Utah as fast as the two of you?" I asked when the spots had receded to a workable place around the corners of my eyes.

"We couldn't say, but I think we're as quick as they come from a parish in Cleveland," volunteered the freckle-splattered one.

There was not an ounce of guile within a ten-mile radius of these dapper-Dan missionaries. And there I stood, untold miles and plenty of years beyond my loss of innocence— God only knew, and possibly these Mormons, how close to the loss of my soul—thinking, *Christ, to be that whole and unfettered again.*

The righteous brothers offered that their main reason for riding so hard came from sleeping three nights in hammocks under thick jungle canopy, where you had to keep your bike helmet on straight through until morning or risk blunt head trauma. "On account of the falling coconuts," said the shorter guy, who had the laser-guided stare of a Tom Cruise performing baptisms for the TV cameras, nodding to the heavens.

This ripped a grin across my still oxygen-deprived face.

"Our hosts, they were dandy people, but we decided to try to reach the beach today," said Freckles.

"We were getting here this afternoon come hell or high water," Cruise added. You could tell he thought this last comment was tethered to the outer banks of naughtiness. That face could have gotten him a three-picture deal if he ever went secular.

We leaned the bikes against palm trees and sprawled on still-warm sand, admiring the setting sun and chatting. Actually, I sprawled while they sat like proper gentlemen in the waning light. This was more a job interview with accountants than chatting. If the Mormons had been my only strange encounter of late it would have remained worth the hard pedal to the water's edge. But these refined riders were simply icing on a rather surreal cake of recent events. What they didn't know? I too was pedaling away from my own point of impact.

"By any chance, you boys run into a guy back in the jungle named Big John Proverb?"

They thought about it for a respectful minute. "We meet a lot of people on our mission," Cruise offered. "That's really the purpose of our being out here. But this acquaintance of yours doesn't ring a bell."

Freckles straightened his tie. "What does he look like?"

It was settled beyond a doubt: They didn't know the dude. At six foot seven and in the neighborhood of 350 pounds soaking wet, Big John was a force of nature, a raised canvas even in Warhol's art gallery of life. To survive the experience of Big John's company was something you wouldn't forget, falling coconuts or not.

"It's hardly important. You guys wouldn't believe me, anyway." I waited, dying for them to take the bait. Clearly, I was looking to stun the Brothers Prim with descriptions of this towering presence I'd stumbled upon while camping near Mayan ruins along the Yucatán Peninsula. This behemoth had eyes that resembled a pair of mirrors for the sun and a dry chuckle that refuted the maxim that time heals all wounds. I needed to see their jaws drop open, their brows furrow, and awe blanket their fresh-scrubbed faces when I dug out the meat and bones of certain unsavory episodes Big John ate up as his daily bread.

Polite to a fault, the Mormons didn't press the subject. Damn them. And since I couldn't interest either spiffy gent in a beer, I pedaled on.

I'd put in the last tent stake when a cloud blotted out the sun. This was strange, since it had been blue skies to the horizon all day. I came off one knee to have a look. It took less than an instant for my adrenaline to spike off the charts. That's when I attempted a spastic karate chop display and simultaneously called out for Momma.

Looming above me, in a working ranch hand's ensemble complete with spurs, black ten-gallon cowboy hat, and a belt buckle wide enough to double as a serving tray at a debutante ball, stood one fierce hombre.

"Hate to be the bearer of bad news, but it's not safe to sleep here," he announced in a clipped midwestern accent.

No shit, was my first thought. If a guy as big as a Buick could ambush me in broad daylight, I was bunking in a terrible spot. But how'd he manage that, anyway? I was tucked away at the edge of the jungle, between skyscraper-size trees and a sloping open field. I thought I'd see and hear someone coming from a healthy distance. He had to be the largest ninja on record, and not wearing the official uniform, either.

"Wh-Where'd you come from?" I stammered, hands still locked in their useless karate chop positions.

I learned in short order that Big John answered only the questions he wanted to; the rest simply drifted harmlessly to the ground around his feet and melted like wet snow.

"It's my job," he said with a shrug of nonchalance. When Big John smiled, his whole demeanor changed. Say anything you want about the guy, but someone had instilled good dental hygiene into this giant's daily regime at an early age.

Recovering a little from outright panic, I said, "You know, I thought ninjas had to be . . . smaller. Like jockeys with better hand-eye coordination."

Again the smile. Maybe I could distract him with humor long enough to make a break for it, Jack-down-the-beanstalk fashion. But another inspection of his arms extinguished any hope. Big John didn't have the cosmetic muscles one achieves from hours in the gym; he was forged out of farmboy-toiling-in-the-field stock. And his proportions were those of someone born on a planet with the gravity of, say, Jupiter. Even his skin seemed to have more in common with *Tyrannosaurus rex* than *Homo sapiens.* But damn, somewhere an advertising exec for Colgate toothpaste was searching in vain for that very set of choppers.

"I'm a bounty hunter, among other things. You learn to be light and still or you go hungry."

Bounty hunter? The term doesn't mean much when you're sitting in the comfort of your own castle, but staring up at one in the flesh from a humid little spot on the rim of the rain forest makes the blood freeze and the toes go clammy. You know that feeling that comes over you when the flashing strobes of a police cruiser light up your rearview mirror? Even when it passes by for another vehicle, you have to cough down the fear. My take on the bounty hunter game was a bunch of cops without badges, training, or restraint. And here was the heavyweight champ of his profession in my proverbial rearview. At the last moment I chose not to share my thoughts on the subject with Big John.

"This is an archaeological site," he informed me. "The Mexican government had a bunch of *federales* protecting it from pot hunters—guys who steal artifacts to sell on the black market. But there were some problems telling the guards from the thieves, so now I keep an eye on it."

I nodded. "You watch the watchdogs."

"No, I'm the only dog now."

It seemed like an awfully large swath of real estate for one man to protect, but if word got out that the man was Big John . . . And he *had* located me in mere moments. We stood in this awkward limbo for a spell. Maybe he was waiting for me to pack up my stuff.

"I'm kinda at a loss here, 'cause it's too late to pedal on down the trail," I said. My hope was he'd allow me to stay, but check in during the night. Sort of like a Mayan ruins neighborhood crime watch.

Big John thought it over. "These pot hunters mean business. If they happen onto you in the middle of the night, it could get dicey." He thought some more. "Gather up your things and follow me."

It weighed on my mind that I was blindly accompanying a colossal man dressed like an extra from the musical *Oklahoma!* I couldn't recall the cast of *Oklahoma!* having 9-mm Glocks tucked in their belts. We traipsed deeper into the jungle, and I started to imagine what my photo would look like on the side of a milk carton.

We stopped at a charred fire circle. John started a nice little blaze before he ushered me farther along a pitifully small path. My panniers kept snagging on roots and branches. Ten minutes later, in another clearing, he lit a second fire, and that one we walked away from as well.

Big John had a stride that covered yards, not feet, with each step, but I soon caught up enough to ask why we couldn't bed down for the night around one of the campfires. It seemed like a reasonable question considering it's a helluva a lot easier to ride a loaded bicycle than push it, and pushing was what I was doing in this thick tropical understory. Fatigue was setting up shop in my legs and shoulders. I scrambled to stay close. It was one of the questions I thought Big John had chosen not to answer. But it turned out to be just a delayed transmission, like I was Apollo 13 and he was Houston.

"It rattles the pot hunters," Big John finally replied. "They come upon warm coals and other traces of me and start thinking I'm everywhere. Maybe they begin to wonder if there's a battalion of stealth warriors working with me, lurking in the canopy somewhere."

I couldn't resist the urge to look over my shoulder, eyeing vines and branches in the dying light.

"Mind games make powerful weapons, don't they?" he added.

Then Big John pushed aside some foliage that was camouflaging an entryway. I would not have seen it in a million years. If there were ever moments in my life that begged for a sound track, this was one of them.

He might have dressed like a Wild West superhero at a cowpoke costume party, but Big John certainly acted every bit the part of a jungle-reconnaissance CEO. Feeling more like a sidekick than a potential victim now—maybe Robin or Tonto—I stashed my bike a few feet inside the cave and followed the big man deeper into his hideout. Weird thing was we started heading up rather than down. Turned out Big John was using one of the Mayan ruins as his fortress. The exterior was completely hidden by dirt, lichen, and plants better proportioned for a time when dinosaurs roamed the earth. We reached a landing that opened onto a stone observation deck. It was like stepping into a scene from one of the *Star Wars* movies, where they're landing at the secret rebel base on the jungle planet.

"Jesus, you can get the drop on anyone rustling around down there," I said.

Big John nodded, unimpressed by my statement of the obvious. His command center was fully stocked: military-issued (or acquired) surveillance equipment, canned foods, a small arsenal of weapons. He handed me some wine in an empty soup can and we settled in for the night.

"You're doing it right," Big John proclaimed.

I wasn't sure if he was referring to the way I held my spoon as I ate my dinner of beans or something else entirely. We'd been listening to the howler monkeys and other nocturnal creatures adding their chorus to the evening program. These were VIP seats, and I was grooving on it more than if we had been sitting in Carnegie Hall for a world premiere. Big John's voice coming through after such a long stretch of silence startled me.

"Seeing the world like you are on a bicycle, I mean. Breezing along without destinations. Some of the stories you've told me . . . it takes balls and imagination."

This from a guy who faced down fugitives. I finished off my beans.

"What do you mean, imagination?"

"Majority of people out there play it safe . . . punch the clock, pass go, collect their two hundred bucks, take two weeks down here or over in Florida. Then put it on a loop for twenty more years. Nothing terrible 'bout that. Noble even if they enjoy what they're doing. But doing it just to avoid failing at a life they really wanted . . . that's kind of diminishing. And it certainly lacks imagination."

I nodded, wondering how to avoid the loop and still be part of society. If I have a tragic flaw, it's that I'm a damn social animal. A friend of mine told me the world is divided into two types of people: those who adored summer camp and those who didn't. I became a camp director.

"Most criminals I've hauled in would be taking an evolutionary leap if they punched a clock, for all the creativity they show," said Big John. "We've got this image of outlaws as rebels, you know, people who think too far outside of convention. My view on it is they can't think of much of anything, so they just try to take."

Big John was offering me some high praise. I felt uncharacteristically awkward and unworthy of it, so I let it lie there between us. Instead I turned the conversation back to him.

"You've gotta have a few stories about masterminds you've hunted down or at least a criminal genius or two that slipped through. The cases that make your hall of fame."

It felt like Big John was deciding to let me into the club or something. He started and stopped several times before taking a deep breath.

"You're a journalist, so when you tell these stories—"

I started to protest, rushing out the standard off-the-record spiel, but Big John batted my words away.

"Hey, I thought good newsmen waited for their subjects to bring up that phrase."

He had a point.

"Like I was saying, when you tell these stories, my only request is that you use my name."

I wasn't expecting that. It's usually the opposite way around.

Big John chuckled.

"It's sort of a stage name, if you hadn't guessed. That and my wardrobe helped me build up a brand back when I was getting started. And it befits the outrageous shit I've seen and questionable things I've done. Don't get me wrong— the one my parents gave me is fine, but I'll bet it makes for terrible copy."

He had a career in print media if he wanted it. And so

the name Big John Proverb and the enigmatic man behind it could live up to any moniker you wanted to hang on him.

"Why keep wearing the outfit, though?"

Big John looked himself over. "Can't really say. It's hard to find stuff in my size. And a guy needs a hat and a belt, right? Maybe it distracts the competition enough to give me an edge."

Truth is, a man in bike clothing has absolutely no cause to throw fashion stones.

━━ ■ ■ ■ ━━

He claimed to have an ex-wife and ten-year-old daughter back in Arizona (a daughter he wanted to see more of, but it was better not to keep going in and out of her life). The more I got to know this tortured giant, the more I thought of our days in the world as tumbling dice.

Big John had played college ball and could have turned pro, but he felt he needed to serve his country in a little police action over in Vietnam. His football coaches, many of them World War II vets, hammered home that the reasons the good old U.S. of A. still existed for him to enjoy were written in blood on the beaches of Normandy and Midway Island.

He could shoot and move light on his feet and was fast . . . a fantastic specimen. Big John possessed such quality that instead of going to the heart of the battle, he found himself sitting in a hot tub surrounded by laughing officers and three demure Vietnamese call girls he'd been assigned to round up for the party. His tour of duty landed him a gig as a bodyguard, which amounted to baby-sitting military brass in Saigon, running down contraband (booze,

Cuban cigars, and much worse), then looking on while officers behaved like petulant Caligulas.

"As if these dipshits' lives merited a minute's thought to the enemy," Big John pointed out. "We were at war, but at least the enemy was out rebuilding supply lines under the cover of darkness, fighting and dying for a country that between dope runs I'd noticed was actually a rather beautiful place when the napalm wasn't falling. It got harder and harder to look my officers in the eye."

Big John grew quiet.

"The guys I trained with were coming home in bags or hanging on to life, maybe attempting to be noble in the face of some very vague reasons. My officers, on the other hand, referred to casualties as 'decommissioned units' and felt this police action was a big hoot in the jungle. Closest they ever got to danger was when they flew at high altitude over a hot spot on their way to dinner with a general or when one caught a case of the clap."

We listened to the jungle, and I felt a damp mist settling through the high branches. Big John didn't seem to notice.

"They tossed around lives like so many yard darts at a backyard barbecue. No one claimed to know what else to do, while the administration back home couldn't find the definition of 'mission creep' in the dictionary."

It took all of Big John's willpower not to kill the morons he was paid to protect. He sucked it up day by day, and when his tour ended without his having to "decommission" or injure a soul in the name of God and country, Big John hit the States with a plan that included serving in a way he hadn't been allowed to do during his sojourn in the Pacific Rim.

"I became a bounty hunter and put all the techniques I'd acquired tracking down black-market shit in Asia into sniffing out bail jumpers and the occasional bad-ass wherever they took me."

There's balls and imagination for you.

This was the middle of the freewheeling disco decade, so John found plenty of work. He built a reputation for getting the job done quickly and cleanly. When he confronted his quarries, they usually surrendered without a word—if they weren't begging for mercy or wetting their pants. He found the job took a lot of patience, long hours staking out dives, cultivating well-placed contacts in high and low spots, lots of phone calls, more research than you'd expect, and only a small amount of what could be, on any day, lethal risk. It fit his personality. Big John developed strategies and became comfortable, almost relaxed in his chosen profession . . . and could finally sleep at night.

"Sounds corny, but each time I brought in a jumper running from some crappy thing he'd done to the system or his fellow man, I dedicated the completed file to a fallen soldier I hadn't been allowed to march beside in the jungle."

As a papery yellow moon rose, I heard about counterfeiters so precise and talented it wasn't the money that got them caught, but trails of lavish spending and vanity that allowed him to follow them home. Then John told me a story that broke my heart, about being hired by a Slavic man to find his sister, who had answered a vague ad in a small Ukrainian newspaper for dancers, only to wake up working in a Tel Aviv brothel and watching her passport being burned before her eyes.

"By the time I tracked her to where she'd been pimped, they'd sold her off to one of the sexual bondage boutiques in Asia," Big John said, shaking his head. "I was ready to tear the building down at its foundations. Instead, I grabbed up four other petrified Russian girls—they couldn't have been more than thirteen or fourteen years old—and all the way to a waiting taxi I howled like a wolf whose leg's been torn off in a trap." He smiled. "It helps to be big, but crazy completes the package sometimes." Then the smile turned a little sour. "I never found his sister, though. No closure."

Most of his work involved deadbeat dads, petty thieves, check kiters, and welfare cheats whose idea of hiding from a warrant was either to sleep on the couch at their girlfriend's or watch television in Mom's basement.

"But there was this cowboy who died proper, with his boots on and treasure buried all over Nevada."

Before we could get into that story, Big John felt the need to go on foot patrol. I stayed put and pondered all that I'd heard. If even half of it hovered near the truth, Big John was a walking, talking screenplay whose third act hadn't even been written yet. I set my reporter's pad down, stood, and peered into the darkness below. He was out there making his soundless circuit. There was something almost gentle about Big John. If I had to peg him, I'd say he would have loved summer camp, but they sent him to war instead.

"It's pretty quiet tonight," Big John noted upon his return. He topped off my soup can with more wine and took us back to the Nevada desert. "You ever heard of the Ted Binion case?"

In fact, I had. As a journalist working a busy newsroom in New Mexico, I'd caught a couple of wire stories about the gambler's mystery in Las Vegas—they were calling it "L.V. Confidential."

Binion was an infamous character even by Vegas standards. He'd been co-owner of the Horseshoe Club, a downtown landmark started by his Texas gambler daddy back in the 1940s. A bright ne'er-do-well, scion of the Benny Binion casino dynasty, Ted was the life of the party—eccentric, brash, and something of a honkytonk gangster. It was drug abuse that caused Binion to finally lose his stake in the neon-lit cash cow. The FBI and IRS were after him for years, while he continued playing high roller to the end. He was found dead in a favorite rocking chair at fifty-five, a real Elvis-like scene. His death was considered an accidental overdose at first, and they buried him in grand tradition. An impeached judge delivered the eulogy, and Doors music played as they lowered the casket into the ground.

Then all hell broke loose, or, as Big John put it, that's when the other cowboy boot dropped.

Turned out that Sandy Murphy, Ted's live-in girlfriend, widely described as one part biker bitch and two parts debutante cheerleader, had teamed up with her younger lover, a sharp-dressing ex-con named Rick Tabish, to cause the high roller's untimely demise and make it look like an accident. The man had been employed by Binion, proving that payroll can indeed kill you. That cover-up lasted less than a week. People fled, people got caught and people went to jail—but not before Rick Tabish tried the most audacious stunt since Bugsy Siegel built the town.

Seems that earlier in the year Binion had taken some of his casino earnings and, in classic antiestablishment style, chosen a hole in the desert over banks and deposit boxes. He'd hired Tabish to bury about $5 million in silver coins and bars. Tabish brought along two other men to raid Binion's stash in Pahrump, about sixty miles outside of Vegas. This was at three in the morning, exactly one day after Binion's death. Law enforcement found Tabish using a backhoe to deposit the loot into a dump truck. It was so over-loaded with bars by the time they got there that the truck was buried to its axles under the weight.

"Pigs get fat and hogs get slaughtered," Big John noted. "Here's where I come into this bit of nastiness. I'd done some short-term work for the casino right out of the service—tracking down guests who'd left sizable unpaid tabs—but it didn't suit me. Anyway, a guy said to be connected to the Binion situation gave me a call, asked if I'd be interested in a salvage project. I met the man, and he intimated he was working for Binion's family on the hush-hush. Seems Ted had buried safes and vaults all over the desert, which made sense, since he was said to be worth fifty million dollars and only a fraction of it has surfaced to date."

So it was a scavenger hunt.

"The informant fed me information about potential lo-cations and showed me this key that he said was the skele-ton to all the locks. Believe you me, it's a helluva lot harder to find a box of steel somewhere in the state of Nevada than a jumper leaving what's usually a clumsy trail as he goes."

I sat hunched forward on my box, wondering how this pirate story would end.

"But those bastards back in Saigon always said I could find anything . . . and they were right. I like to think I'm good at what I do," Big John said just above a whisper. "And in this case lucky. Turns out the man, though his information was solid enough to build on, had no ties to the family and lacked even the hint of honor. What's more, he couldn't pay my expenses. So I walked away."

"What's so lucky? You left it all sitting out there for someone else?"

Big John reached into his shirt and produced a key hanging from a thick chain around his neck. "I didn't exactly leave empty-handed."

More than likely I was looking at the key to an airport locker filled with old gym shorts or to the padlocked box I was sitting on that very second. But seeing the waxy moonlight glint off it in the paws of a hulking, past-his-prime bounty hunter with perfect teeth . . . well, that sent a sweet little shiver down my back. There was only the slimmest of chances I wasn't being shined on, but the thought of Big John lumbering away with a fortune made a flawless parting shot. Of course, the journalist in me couldn't let it fade to black and roll credits.

"Few things I don't get." I held up my pen and paper. "Why tell me?"

"In my estimation, if you sent the population of Tucson across Nevada with shovels, they'd have a better chance of striking oil, water, or both at the same time. Binion's legend is so huge that already folks are calling backhoes their family vehicles so they can dig for his gold on Sunday drives. You asked if I had any good cases. This one's at the top of the heap. Writing a story will only send a few more shovels into the dirt. Good exercise for them."

We locked eyes.

"I never tire of watching people try to wrap themselves around the unbelievable. You have the same expression of disbelief every bail jumper sports when I snatch him back into custody."

"What about the guy you took the key from?" I countered.

"I've made some friends in law enforcement over the years. Now he's just a man without a key and an abundance of official types strip-searching his life from dawn to dusk."

"Nice," I said. True or not, I appreciated that image. I swirled around the dregs at the bottom of my soup can. "Does the key work?"

He grinned. "The right question would be, what am I doing down here if it does?"

I waited.

"One thing I've learned is that we all get caught. I've spent a lifetime watching my back, but not a minute looking over my shoulder." He nodded. "I'm still mulling over whether it would be worth it."

That night I lay down a few feet from a lion of a man and fell into a dreamless slumber, the safe, deathlike sleep of a caveman running on nothing more than primal life support, until the morning brought me back around. We parted over the cold remains of his first campfire, close to where we'd met, Big John checking out my bicycle while I repacked some loose gear.

"By the time I was fourteen they were having to custom-build frames for me," he said.

This didn't come as a surprise.

"It was getting expensive. That's when I started enjoying the sound my football helmet made when I tackled someone just right."

Clearly he wasn't built for distance bike racing, but it

would have been glorious—and slightly grotesque—to see Big John just once in a quarter-mile sprint.

"Any advice for a humble pilgrim trying not to get caught?" I asked, half joking.

Big John put on his hat.

"Don't look at me for wisdom. The Mayans, they were said to be wise beyond measure, and all that's left of them is little more than what you're standing on."

We shook hands.

"Wait, here's something. You listening? Always look to the left of your right-hand man."

"Because?"

"Because it's from that side he'll draw his firearm."

"But if he's your right-hand man . . . ?"

Big John started to walk away. "That's why I work alone."

A few moments later the jungle swallowed him whole, and I was left with a long, hot pedal to the coast.

SIGN LANGUAGE

THE MANAGER HAS PERSONALLY
PASSED ALL THE WATER SERVED HERE

This declaration was proudly displayed in big letters across the top of a sample menu and neatly taped to the door of the restaurant at eye level. I stood over my handlebars in front of the Acapulco eatery, immobilized.

The sun was trying to set on another stellar day in paradise, and this little nugget of humor was icing on my road-weary cake. When I could stop laughing I was left to decide just how to proceed. By the looks of it, they had searched out the largest Magic Marker in the hemisphere to create some unintentional comic relief. Their efforts would have been better served tracking down a translator skilled in the pitfalls and double meanings of the English language—a retired politician, maybe? The goal, to reassure skittish tourists that the water in this restaurant was perfectly safe to drink, succeeded only in conjuring up an image of some bored and rumpled manager sporting a *mucho grande* bladder, standing over the water pitchers, pants down, drinking and peeing his way through countless glasses of water. Hey, it's a living, *compadres*, but really, when do I get bumped down to busboy?

I locked up my bike and ventured in for a table. But just to be safe, I ordered cola, no ice, with my meal.

For me, language is as intoxicating as grain alcohol and equally dangerous. Origins, roots, those word-a-day calendars that people wrap up for Christmas when they can't think of what else to give, the perfect turn of a phrase—it's all music to my ears. What can happen to those melodies in the wrong hands, the tortured wail of signs and billboards on many of the roads I've pedaled down, becomes the literary equivalent of a comic opera. Well-intentioned advertising, bloopered billboards, misinformation spelled across magnetic-lettered marquees, and hastily scribbled messages taped to community bulletin boards have brought me more moments of giddy rapture than one bike rider deserves. At some point I began writing them down. No—I remember exactly where and when I became a secretary for the Society of Sign Language Abuse.

The note on the screen door of the shop boasted:

WE CAN FIX ANYTHING

Inches away, taped above the ringer, was this:

PLEASE KNOCK HARD—BELL DOESN'T WORK

Having exhausted all of my mechanical skills, I really needed someone else to take a crack at the brakes on my bicycle, but when the shop owner arrived, I simply queried him for some unnecessary directions and rolled on down the road, my guess being that brakes are slightly more complicated than doorbells.

Once I began my sign language journals, the world became one sprawling linguistic game preserve. Along some of those less-than-exciting stretches of road—which the long-distance cyclist knows far too well, forced to pedal through many a mono-cultured urban jungle and rest at one faceless gas station after another, I started fancying myself a big-time hunter, riding along the asphalt, keeping an eye always peeled for a misplaced word that I could bag for posterity . . . and quality entertainment value.

It's often space limitations that get perfectly coherent sign writers into trouble—that and the lack of an extra magnetic letter or a period in the supply box. Sign writing on marquees is pretty hard on your neck, and nearly impossible if you don't have one of those patented long poles with a strong pickup magnet on the end. I know these things only because my bike travels once landed me a place to sleep above a movie theater in British Columbia.

Steven Sutter, the bucolic owner/manager/projectionist/marquee writer, was a brother in the wheel-and-pedal game. He invited me to bed down in the projection room of his vintage-style two-screen theater. It was warmth, a roof over my head, excellent company, enough free popcorn and soda to make me plenty sick, and a marathon of classic horror flicks to boot. On the big screen that evening and well into the night were *Rosemary's Baby, The Fog,* and the cheesiest of zombie masterpieces, *Dawn of the Dead* (shot in a mall outside my other childhood home of Pittsburgh).

The fee for such a memorable evening was to help Steve change the marquee before the weekend customers drove by on their Friday-morning commute. We were up at dawn, freezing our fingers to the bone and spelling out titles and stars' names in something close to a universally accepted marquee shorthand.

"There are very few verbs, the occasional preposition like *in,* and you use the star's last name only, unless they are complete unknowns," Steve instructed. He was speaking to me with the intensity of a blacksmith mentoring his only son on how not to scar himself with molten iron or drop the anvil on his shin. I found it fascinating, though perhaps the lesson was wasted on the likes of me. Steve favored teaching through example. I'd put up a few innocent words, but with a few quick strokes of the magnet he was able to create all manner of absurdity.

He shared an embarrassing moment from his past with me. "I once made the colossal mistake of writing out Clint Eastwood's name before full light one morning. Everyone's favorite Dirty Harry ended up as a female body part. I got calls on that one. Boy, did my phone ever ring. If I had that sort of customer response to my weekly movies, I'd be living somewhere warm—like Cancun. Most people wanted to know if I'd gone into the porno biz."

Such shorthand bloopers turned out to be the meat and potatoes of my journal entries. A doctor's office in Idaho provided me with this solid gem:

SPECIALIST IN WOMEN AND OTHER DISEASES

I'm figuring his business fell off significantly when this sign went up—at least among his female customers.

A store outside of Newport, Oregon, announced:

GOD BLESS MAPLE LOGS AND APPLE STRUDEL

It was meant to be two signs, but lack of space can be deadly to the marquee writer. Hell, I've also found maple logs and apple strudel to be little morsels of heaven to a tired rider on the road, but who knew they were actually blessed by the divine?

A church in Iowa seemed to be taking two steps forward and three steps back in their children's programming with this one:

SCOUTS ARE SAVING CANS/BOTTLES TO BE RECYCLED. PROCEEDS USED TO CRIPPLE CHILDREN.

That couldn't be good for recruiting new members. Maybe the notorious skating femme fatale Tonya Harding was at the helm of their fund-raising program.

And a tried-and-true classic:

SLOW CHILDREN AHEAD

Every time I see this one, and I've spied it in multiple countries, I wonder if I'm the only person who thinks it's crying out for a comma, a dash, something.

As long as there are marquees, impaired signs will continue to breed like rabbits. A bar in Mexico offered up this drink deal:

SPECIAL COCKTAILS FOR THE LADIES WITH NUTS

A dentist's office in Venezuela trying to cater to English-speakers, and what appeared to be those with specific religious preferences, made this reaching promise:

TEETH EXTRACTED BY THE LATEST METHODISTS

And the unfortunate choice of shorthand on a public TV station's billboard nearly caused me to pedal through a red light:

I UPPED MY PLEDGE—UP YOURS

At least I would have died laughing as the cars flattened me. My first thought: *PBS certainly is going for something of an edgier, World Wrestling–type crowd these days.*

According to my entry, a house of prayer in Ohio posted this on their billboard:

DON'T LET WORRY KILL YOU. LET THE CHURCH HELP.

Everyone from Joan of Arc to the entire supporting cast of the Spanish Inquisition would certainly offer up a resounding amen to that one.

Sometimes errors and creative phrasing would pop up in mild-mannered marketing pamphlets for hotels and resorts. In New Zealand I once rounded a bend only to gaze upon a majestic oasis. Glorious. While reading through their brochure at the gatehouse, I was amused by this particular line:

FAMOUS FOR ITS PEACE AND QUIET,
CROWDS FROM ALL OVER THE WORLD
FLOCK HERE TO ENJOY THE SOLITUDE.

Written by an exuberant salesperson wanting it both ways, no doubt. That line caused me such a laughing fit, I stumbled off my bike. And what about the rancher just a few miles up the road from that very resort? He'd posted an equally preposterous note on his fence:

NO TRESPASSING WITHOUT PERMISSION

Maybe the same guy who penned the hotel brochure had been doing some moonlighting, passing himself off as a crackerjack sign writer to residents.

One thing that I've discovered during my travels is that a great place to make camp for the night is a cemetery. Maybe that sounds sacrilegious, but consider this: As long as you're not the type of person who gets creeped out easily, it's a quiet, safe night's sleep in a spot where you won't be disturbed by anyone else getting up to use the bathroom. Cemeteries also have a disproportionately high number of laugh-out-loud signs. I know, I'm going straight to hell for these statements, no pit stop in purgatory, but who could disagree with some of my findings?

This was posted on the front gate of a cemetery in Ireland:

PEOPLE ARE RESTRICTED FROM PICKING FLOWERS FROM ANY BUT THEIR OWN GRAVES

A buddy of mine who cycled Russia told me I might want to avoid a certain Moscow burial spot based on this declaration:

YOU ARE WELCOME TO VISIT THE CEMETERY WHERE FAMOUS COMPOSERS, ARTISTS, AND WRITERS ARE BURIED DAILY

Clearly, my friend had me mistaken for an author of higher standing, but it didn't sound like that cemetery was a big supporter of the arts.

And another gem taped across a beverage stand at the entrance to a cemetery in California was so over the top that I had to spend money on a cup, and I don't even drink java as a rule:

OUR COFFEE'S STRONG ENOUGH TO WAKE THE DEAD.
WON'T COST YOU AN ARM OR A LEG, EITHER.

Then there are folks I think I would have enjoyed tipping back a few cold ones with, based on their headstones:

HOW COME IT'S SO HOT,
AND WHAT AM I DOING IN THIS BASKET?

I GUESS THAT WASN'T JUST ANOTHER HEAD COLD

RIGHT PEDAL GAS, LEFT PEDAL BRAKE

ONLY THE GOOD DIE YOUNG

(on the grave of Ezekiel Aikle, age 102)

And my favorite:

YOUR AD HERE. SEE MY RELATIVES FOR DETAILS!

In my journal, I subtitled this one "Death of the Most Earnest Salesman." Obviously, the guy was an honest-to-goodness closer right to the end . . . and beyond, the exclamation point being his last, inspired act.

Roadside bathrooms are especially good places for the occasional chuckle. Sure, you must wade through a lot of religious bickering done with Magic Markers, a fairly large number of kinky solicitations, and badly drawn stick figure genitalia, but there are some real treasures if you keep scanning the walls. I once had to use the facilities in a gorgeous public office in Auckland, New Zealand. When I arrived at the stall I was confronted by this troubling message:

TOILET OUT OF ORDER. PLEASE USE FLOOR BELOW.

More than a few people had taken them up on their kind offer. I nearly slipped on the wet surface but held myself upright and other things in for a little while longer while I worked my way gingerly down a flight of stairs to more proper facilities.

In a truckstop outside of Quanari, Texas, I noted that not everyone was charmed by the whole roping-and-ranching mind-set of the Lone Star State. It would explain why they'd drawn an arrow to those sanitary toilet seat covers with this invitation:

LOOK, FREE COWBOY HATS, YEEHAW . . . TAKE ONE

I was especially tickled by the person who turned a nasty bit of wordplay into a good laugh across the wall of a roughneck bar in Australia. Someone had scrawled:

I SCREWED YOUR MOTHER!

Right under this, in another color marker, was the rock-solid advice:

GO HOME, DAD, YOU'RE DRUNK AGAIN

In a mad dash to the safety of a toilet seat in British Columbia, I still had to take a second to appreciate the clever placement of a familiar sticker applied to the wall above:

FASTEN SEATBELT WHEN LIGHT IS ON
IN CASE OF A WATER EVACUATION YOUR SEAT
WILL ACT AS A FLOTATION DEVICE

And the king of commode comedy made it into my journal via a crowded public bathroom in Indonesia. The sign stated:

FOR YOUR CONVENIENCE, WE RECOMMEND
COURTEOUS, EFFICIENT SELF-SERVICE

Exactly what in the hell were they trying to tell people with a sign like this, and why was it written in English? Had management run into trouble with First World tourists loitering around this airless, stench-filled room just waiting for someone else to give their business a final shake or wipe their bums for them? I had to roll my bike right into the tight bathroom with me for fear it might have been swallowed up by the masses of humanity in the streets, so efficient I was not, but courteous and self-serviced? Absolutely.

━━━━ ■ ━━━━

Let's call it a sign of our politically correct times, but you don't see as many bumper stickers these days—outside of such liberal hotbeds as Santa Cruz, California, Portland, Oregon, and Austin, Texas, that is, where tolerance is the law and all those who don't like it can just move the hell on down the road. But take a bike tour that keeps you on the road for several months and your faith in man's ability to express a four- to six-word opinion across chrome will be restored. Though less common, these nuggets of wisdom are still alive and well for anyone to see out there on the world's highways and byways.

Road rage be damned. I for one can't get enough of these little bullets of humor and pop psychology. If I have to choke on all that exhaust, I might as well get a laugh out of it. Of the hundreds of entries in my journals, here's my first team. We'll call it Metal Cowboy's Hall of Fame.

In no particular order:

1. Vegetarian: ancient Indian word meaning "bad hunter."
2. I considered atheism, but there weren't enough holidays.
3. Your sole purpose in life might simply be to serve as a warning to others.
4. I want to die peacefully in my sleep like Grandfather . . . not screaming in terror like his passengers.
5. I'm in shape. Round *is* a shape.
6. Where there's a will, I want to be in it.
7. I found Jesus! He was in my trunk when I got back from Tijuana.
8. A smoking section in a restaurant is a little like a peeing section in a pool.
9. We have enough youth. What about a fountain of smart?
10. I can't remember—am I the good twin or the evil twin?
11. I couldn't repair your brakes, so I made your horn louder.
12. Jesus saves sinners . . . and redeems them for cash and valuable prizes.
13. The more I learn about terrorism, the more I understand the phone company.
14. Some days it's just not worth gnawing through the straps.
15. Lord, I pray you'll save me from your followers.
16. A fool and his money . . . can throw one helluva party.

Ain't that the truth. And I've certainly been one such merry fool on more than a few occasions. But here's the thing: Until someone came up with the concept of bumper stickers, I considered Henry Ford's little invention a total write-off. On most days I still do, but I can laugh about it while pedaling by traffic now.

Having spent quality time gathering all these phrases, misspellings, and signs of confusion, I stumbled upon a pair of proclamations that when put together were so radiant I was forced to write them down and give them a place of honor inside my wallet. Some people wear medical alert bracelets, but in my case, if the worst were to happen and my crumpled bike and lifeless carcass are found mashed into the road somewhere, I hope they also locate this note when rifling through my wallet.

I first saw these phrases at a youth hostel in Canada, but I didn't stick them inside my wallet until after a close call with a bus in Mexico. The first part, an inspiring message of the summer camp counselor variety, had been written across the kitchen chalkboard by the hostel manager, one of those annoying early risers who act far too perky before breakfast. It read:

DANCE LIKE NOBODY'S WATCHING
LOVE LIKE IT'S THE FIRST TIME
WORK LIKE YOU DON'T NEED THE MONEY

After he'd whistled out of the room, along shuffled this semiconscious, shirtless Swede. With a cup of coffee in one hand, not missing a beat, the bleary-eyed traveler picked up the chalk and scratched out a classic retort:

DANCE LIKE YOUR FEET HURT
LOVE LIKE YOU NEED THE MONEY
ONLY WORK WHEN PEOPLE ARE WATCHING

You can't buy a moment like that at any price. It takes riding your bike a very long distance, and no small amount of luck.

Now, if I do go out in a blaze of screeching wheels and unchecked velocity, I want it to be a priest or possibly a paramedic who unfolds my little note, a hard guy with a heart that's seen so much pain and suffering that it may have deadened his ability to find easy laughter. The smile that would surely form on his lips with this, my perfect parting shot. He'd walk away comfortable with the knowledge that I didn't take it all too seriously. I enjoyed this absurd ride through the back roads of life like nobody's business. That, and I was never much of a dancer.

RIDING WITH
THE BOSS

Emanuel stood by the bank of a swollen river deep in Peru, a pair of black saucers for eyes and a crooked grin beckoning me to his dugout canoe. The rain, warm and steady, played a backbeat on my bike helmet as I weighed my options. Though there were several other makeshift water taxi services dotting the muddy shore, I was drawn to Emanuel for his loopy smile. But what really closed the deal? Not the price or seaworthiness of his skiff, but the young man's choice in T-shirts.

"You like the Boss?" I asked, pointing at his mint-condition silkscreen of Bruce Springsteen from the *Born to Run* tour. Emanuel nodded his head enthusiastically, then turned his attention to my gear. I probably could have asked Emanuel if he was a fan of Lawrence Welk and received the same response. I told myself to put aside that American-centric mind-set and entertain the thought that my escort actually could be a discerning fan of the Asbury Park hero. He might even know that his shirt was no throwaway piece of mass merchandise from the overblown *Born in the USA* tour but a truly vintage tee that could whip up a nasty little bidding war on eBay. I glanced at the shirt again, and memories rushed in hard and fast. It had once hung in my own closet and pedaled with me down the bumpy roads of my adolescence.

Emanuel helped lift my bike into the canoe, and seconds later we were afloat.

"Cuánto cuesta el T-shirt?" I asked, like everything was for sale near the equator. I caught the nasty odor of an ugly American seeping through my intrepid-adventurer façade. But this could not be helped—I wanted that shirt in the worst way. It was a talisman, a portal to another time, when every day held promise, songs on the radio spoke directly to me, and each girl I brushed against offered countless reasons to believe.

Either he hadn't heard me or was thinking it over. I tried again.

"I'll give you twenty American dollars for your shirt."

Those black saucers widened a bit as Emanuel tried to contain his loopy grin. He understood what I was asking just fine. He held his ground, offering a shrug that provided no answer. He gunned the throttle as I steadied myself.

"No sale," Emanuel answered cheerfully.

This kid had yet to fully embrace the engine of capitalism. He looked all of thirteen. Like most people, when I was thirteen years old I didn't give a damn about business either. All I wanted was to be someone else.

Sure, appearances had something to do with it. The usual stuff: garden-variety pimples, a complete lack of facial hair, and the scantest trace of buttocks. My smile carried with it the imminent threat of braces. Also, I had feathered hair so blond and fine that women—the wrong women, grandmothers with raspy voices and lunchroom ladies sporting hair nets and those clear plastic gloves—

would brazenly reach out for a touch, just a little pet or gentle tug.

"That is one gorgeous head of hair, sweetie," came the throaty chorus sung by well-meaning but unwittingly sadistic ladies. "It's like the purest silk woven together with . . . that's it, platinum."

Just what every freshman navigating the social battlefield of high school wants broadcast in a public setting. Granted, it was the 1970s, when the outrageous hairdos of heartthrobs like Peter Frampton and Shaun Cassidy roamed the earth with impunity, but believe me when I say that a young man's do *can* be too pretty.

And let's not forget a growth spurt that left me nearly seven inches taller but so damn lean that between the height and hair color, my nickname on the basketball team was Q-Tip. They even silkscreened it across the back of my uniform without prior consent. I picked up my game jersey at the locker room window and had a decision to make. When saddled with a humiliating handle—say, that of a product used to remove wax from the ear canal—it's better to play along with the joke, take detailed notes, and seek revenge at a later date.

The other reason I wanted out of my skin at the time was that in my arrogant, testosterone-addled mind, my body was becoming far too crowded for the vast reservoir of knowledge I possessed. I was not immune to what every person believes at age thirteen—that you will keep getting smarter and stronger until the sun folds upon itself and the universe goes numb, and furthermore, your thoughts, words, and deeds are gospel. This condition passes sometime after graduation, usually during your first job in the real world. If it persists, though, you'll have no choice but to become a politician.

I also nurtured a solid case of teenage angst, and what fueled my rage on a daily basis was that I had absolutely nothing to be angry about. I suspect it's how the Clash felt after their album *London Calling* went platinum. It's hard to be rich *and* punk.

Who would I have traded places with at the time? Without question, linebacker Franco Harris during the Immaculate Reception play that sent the Pittsburgh Steelers to the Super Bowl, but only if I couldn't have been Bruce Springsteen, roughneck prince of the Jersey shore, the poet king of rock and roll. Elvis possessed hips and hair, but the Boss has syntax and knows how to front a live show that *Rolling Stone,* my bible at the time, called a complete religious experience. Pass the collection plate—I was ready to pry open my wallet, kneel, and give thanks to the Garden State for letting their native son travel.

Prior to seeing Springsteen, my live concert resumé included a Jimmy Buffett benefit for the manatees and a horrendous Four Tops tribute at a county fairground, at which I don't believe one original member of the Tops was present (my mom had won the tickets for this "event" at a church social). So it's a wonder the unfiltered rush of Bruce's rock-and-roll fury didn't kill me on the spot. I once mocked the TV images of screaming girls losing it over the Beatles, but when the Boss did "Jungleland" for an encore, I wept from the third row without a second thought.

This brief, ethereal escape from the confines of my

wispy thirteen-year-old frame nearly never happened. A homeroom cutie named Stephanie Cahill almost ruined the glory that is Springsteen live.

I'd spend entire class periods staring into the distance and contemplating various and unsuspecting parts of her body: an ankle here, her forearm as the sun spotlighted it during American history. The poison in my gonads even persuaded me to throw over one of my best pals and offer Stephanie my remaining precious ticket to the sold-out concert. Odds were she didn't actually like me but was incapable of controlling her flirt mechanism yet. I received mixed signals but chose to ignore all such information. In junior high, a ticket to a rock show at the stadium, on a weeknight no less, would land all but the worst geeks and shop-class gargoyles a date. We knew some of the same people, so it wasn't social suicide for her to be seen in my company. But, lacking transportation beyond my bicycle, we agreed to meet in the parking lot. It was understood that if I failed to bring along substantial quantities of alcoholic refreshments, I'd be lower than pond scum and treated as such. Standard procedure.

Even though my gang, Jon, Carl, Scott, and Derrick, had been shafted of this rare chance to see the Boss, they helped me obtain liquor and beer for the date. It's a bedrock of the teenage boy's code of conduct. We slouched over our bikes in Derrick's alley, drinking a portion of the spoils from our parents' cabinets and rec room fridges. That's the evening we discovered that peach brandy should *never* be cut with Pepsi.

Derrick had older brothers, so he was our pack's mentor. He turned us on to the newest fads, bootleg stuff, and basically corrupted us before we could corrupt ourselves. And always, always he was five minutes cooler than whatever he was showing us.

We ragged on our school for a while and argued the validity of this new band called the Knack before talk came around to my impending date.

"Stephanie's a tease. Worse, that uptight bitch probably thinks the E Street Band is a kid's group on *Sesame Street.*" Jon was the most bitter. For the record, though, he referred to everyone as some sort of bitch—uptight, fine, lazy, tired— regardless of his mood. For Jon, life was a bitch, plain and simple. It had a lot to do with being born shortly after his sister, who lit up every space so brightly that my friend lived in a perpetual shadow. We'd spent the previous weekend locked in his room listening to *The River,* Springsteen's holiday-timed release that was anything but ho-ho-ho happy music. "Ain't that a bitch!" Jon purred occasionally from behind his headphones. If we could have shot the two-album set directly into our veins, it might have fought off for another hour or two the fury of being thirteen.

"It's still not too late to leave that pesky bitch at the turnstiles and take along someone who'd appreciate the moment," Jon said.

Carl threw an empty bottle over the fence and said it was time to roll. His dad had been in Vietnam, so everywhere we went, Carl took point, acting as though we were headed into hostile territory. Scott, usually as quiet as Miles Davis offstage, liked to point out that Carl's dad had only been a photographer in 'Nam, not a commanding officer.

"Who's braver, a guy seeing action with a gun or a camera?" Carl came back with.

Harsh. But then, most of junior high was fought behind enemy lines. I think we were tough on each other because everyone else was going to be even tougher.

My pals were escorting me to the stadium parking lot—mainly because we went everywhere together, but also to crash any tailgate parties that didn't notice us nipping food and pocketing beers as we went.

Our route followed Bayshore Boulevard, a glorious stretch of unbroken sidewalk and a seawall to keep from spinning into the water twenty feet below. Heat lightning popped now and again over the horizon miles offshore. It lit up the night sky like a Renaissance painting. Winter in Florida. We were wearing only T-shirts and still sweating as we pedaled the quiet causeway.

When we rode as a group there was one speed, fast, and only one rule: Run all stop signs unless otherwise instructed. We jumped curbs and zagged around parked cars with the daredevil nonchalance of boys coming into their full. The bikes were merely extensions of our bodies and the streets our playground.

"If the Knack were here right now, I'd beat them like they owed me money," Derrick announced from the front of the line. Unless it was Led Zeppelin, Aerosmith, or Black Sabbath, Derrick couldn't be bothered.

"What about Devo?" I asked. "Would you pummel them?"

"Freaks," replied Derrick, sounding eerily like his dad on the subject of Led Zeppelin.

"Least new wave isn't disco," Jon noted.

We offered up a collective moment of silence. Only the sound of freewheels spinning and gears clicking could be heard though the darkness. Disco received my gang's most vocal scorn. Jon couldn't even touch the topic for fear he'd start hyperventilating. My dark secret: Sometimes I broke into dance to "I Will Survive" in front of my bedroom mirror and found myself humming "Gloria" in the shower. Life's a mystery. I tried to loathe the inferno that was disco, from ABBA to the Village People, but I couldn't be trusted to turn it off. It had a beat even a skinny white boy could dance to, and teen angst aside, who couldn't help but smile when Donna Summer let it fly?

My gang coasted through three lights without breaking formation, skating through the yellows each time and not changing our pace line by a stroke. Finally Carl yelled into the night sky just because it was there, broke rank, and ped-aled ahead.

We spun the final mile to the stadium as Jon belted out Tom Petty's "American Girl." *Please, God, let mine be waiting in the parking lot with her hair and her guard down.* Through a sea of Trans Ams and Grand Torinos we located Stephanie, but it appeared others were also on the case. Her posse of gal pals was scattered around, as expected . . . along with two brutes in letterman jackets. Jocks from high school—a combination I couldn't compete with yet. Though they were two years older at the most, with cars and facial hair they might as well have been another species.

"Bet those no-neck bitches love disco," Jon announced, softly enough to avoid getting our asses kicked before we'd parked the bikes. We chained the two-wheeled fleet to streetlight poles and shuffled toward Stephanie and com-pany.

I mustered up as much confidence as I could for a guy

nicknamed Q-Tip. Greetings were grunted all around, beer was distributed, and I claimed my position by standing beside my date.

It went downhill from there.

The jocks took the highly original tack of making fun of our bicycles even as they drank our brew. Stephanie was forced to pretend we were together so she could get into the concert, but beyond that I held as much appeal as a blouse her mom bought her from the junior-miss rack at JC Penney. Even with her superior powers of flirtation, Stephanie's body language alone said the jocks were her holy grail. It wasn't like I was asking for a girl who laughed for no one else, but a little eye contact would have been nice. The jocks didn't have an extra ticket, or my gang and I would have been drinking alone already.

With a few misleading song references, Carl determined that these letterman-clothed interlopers knew less about Springsteen than Stephanie did. A travesty. It spiraled into a pissing match, with Carl challenging everyone to shotgun beers in rapid succession. It was then he stumbled into one of the jocks and, just like that, my pals were no longer welcome at the party. Stephanie whispered something into the fallen jock's ear, and I felt more and more like the odd man out. But what could I do? She smelled like morning flowers, so I just stood there and drank beer. Once inside, she'd send me to the snack bar or excuse herself to go to the rest room, and I'd be solo at the rock show—a fate worse than death to any teenager.

But I was wrong—a fate worse still is arriving at the turnstiles only to realize you've lost your tickets. They'd been in my wallet when I'd left the house. Before I could think it through I was sliced in half by Stephanie's mascara-laced evil eye of epic proportions. She looked like Pat Benatar on PCP. This had the potential to set my dating career back years. The jocks swooped in to the rescue, saying they'd flip a coin and give up one of their tickets or try to scalp a third for her. I slipped away at that point, not interested in how it would end.

The final insult came when I went for my bike. It must have been moved by my pals as a joke, or they'd carted it home somehow as retribution for not standing up for them with the jocks. I was buzzed but certain this was where we'd locked them. The first chords by the opening band, mixed with muffled cheers, could be heard coming from inside the stadium. It was a five-mile walk home. I wanted to cry.

"Psst . . . get over here, you sorry bitch." Jon, Carl, Scott, and Derrick were hiding behind a Goodwill Industries donation trailer.

Scott fanned out a fistful of Springsteen tickets, and the guys broke up like it was the funniest thing in the world.

"Taking your pair of tickets was my idea," Jon said. "I grabbed them out of your wallet back in the alley when you were paying me for the Pepsi, just in case Stephanie turned superficial like we knew she would."

Stealing the jocks' tickets, on the other hand, had been an inspired piece of impromptu lunacy Carl cooked up after his third beer.

"That pinhead kept showing Stephanie their seat numbers, so I knew you were done for. I watched what pocket they went back in, then pinched 'em during the beer-fall stunt." Carl shrugged. "Come on, a few beers doesn't even make me wobbly."

Scott grabbed the tickets. "Couldn't let them crowd out your evening. Besides, they're assholes who don't deserve the privilege." He looked around after he said it. It was easy to talk tough with your pals. "Let's hide the bikes, find a gate on the other side of the stadium, and see ourselves a little rock-and-roll opera," he added.

Derrick hung back. Damn it, we were still short a ticket.

"Forget about me. Springsteen's a little too throaty, anyway. I'm heading home, maybe crank up the Zep." We watched Derrick pedal away, a selfless hero to the hard-rock cause.

As much as we wanted to take in the sight of two red-faced jocks ripping out the bucket seats of their semi-restored Chevy Nova, searching in vain for those tickets while Stephanie's tears made her makeup run, we couldn't risk it.

If a concert can actually change a person at the molecular level, the Boss's did that to me. I was transformed, released from the chains of my waking life and allowed a glimpse of what I might become if I just held on. It felt as though I'd downed a fifth of hundred-proof adrenaline. My fingertips tingled, and everything made sense.

A gentle rain began to fall as we coasted out of the stadium lot. I took in a lungful of damp night air and closed my eyes, feeling the rain on my face as I held my head back and gained velocity. This was living.

Suddenly there was a squealing noise, and the Nova left fifty yards of rubber as it blasted across the lot. Evidently the jocks had figured out what had happened to their tickets. But the dumbshits gave us a head start.

Carl slipped right into military-speak. His tone bordering on glee, he yelled, "Split up and rally at Bravo checkpoint"—the alley behind our school. It's not a party till someone tries to run you down with an 8-cylinder engine.

Jon went with me, while Carl and Scott spun off in the opposite direction. A soundtrack of Springsteen gems—"Racing in the Street," "Thunder Road," "Born to Run," and "Darkness on the Edge of Town"—rattled around in my head as we shot down driveways and cut through yards. Dogs barked everywhere, kitchen lights popped on as we dodged garbage cans, Serpicoed through a mall parking lot, and pedaled madly for the cover provided by an interstate overpass. The jocks never really had a chance.

An hour later we'd regrouped behind the school and were embellishing our bravery.

When we ran out of stories Jon said, "We're gonna have to watch our backs for a few weeks."

There was a moment of silence that carried a slight hint of dread.

"Okay, a few years. And hope maybe those Nova-driving bitches break a bone or two on roller disco night." Wanted men now, we laughed more than was necessary.

"It was worth it, though," I said.

The gang thought that one over in complete silence.

"Hell, yeah," Jon confirmed.

"Hell, yeah," we replied in unison.

You're only thirteen once. I fell asleep with my headphones on that night, "Born to Run" looping on the stereo.

■ ■ ■

Emanuel had delivered me safely to the other side. It was time to pay the ferry man.

"You sure you won't sell me that T-shirt?"

He shook off my obscene American purchasing power, again with the shrug. This time, however, he smelled the shirt in exaggerated fashion to indicate it was soiled and not fit for resale—the subtext being that my request was even too foolish for him to make a quick buck on.

"I know where can you get your own."

I waited for the punch line, but Emanuel was serious. He provided me with directions of a sort to the market in the next sizable town, where I was to count to the fourth aisle off the square and look for a family selling lots of tapes and CDs. The beauty of a bicycle adventure is the fluidity of one's days. If I wanted to go on a wild-goose chase after an elusive old concert T-shirt thirty miles to the west, there was absolutely no one aboard to talk me out of it. My plan for Peru had always been to pass through en route to points further south. While the landscape of the country was without parallel, the politics of the place, specifically of the Shining Path guerrillas, were without mercy on an American traveling the wrong road.

I gave Emanuel the extra twenty anyway, for his steadfast resistance of materialism, and went in search of my T-shirt. Hey, you can only die at the hands of political fanatics once.

My search took the better part of two days, but the satisfaction of standing in front of all those vintage concert tees was palpable. This was an absolute gold mine. It appeared, from my side of the table, that every major and most of the minor tours of two decades were represented—from Guns N' Roses to Boston, Whitney Houston to a rare Live Aid two-tone baseball-style tee. True to his word, Emanuel had directed me to Peru's largest stash of Springsteen shirts. At pennies on the dollar, my only concern was how many I could buy and safely carry on the bike. Maybe I'd ship a box or three of various artists back to the States . . . or cut a deal for cases and cases. The plan forming between my ears placed me at the helm of a vast rock-and-roll memorabilia empire. I'd auction products online and in the back of magazines, never flooding the market, keeping demand high. I reverently lifted a few of the crisp Springsteen shirts so I could find a larger size.

That's when the dream fell apart.

I kept digging, but the sizes never went beyond adult smalls. If anything, they seemed to slide into children's fits. I held up a shirt, stretched it out as far as possible without tearing it, and still the thing wouldn't clear my neck. That's when I slumped down between a stack of CDs and a box of Red Hot Chili Peppers—the band, not the vegetable. Fool's gold, brothers and sisters. Unless I wanted to open up a rock-and-roll day care center or outfit the Seven Dwarves, I was done.

The demure merchant smiled at me from behind a Journey tee. At least I'd solved the age-old mystery of where tiny concert T-shirts go to die. A crowd of curious folks who would fit easily into any of the shirts I was clutching began to gather around my bicycle. Time to go myself. I got on my ride, then came off again. What the hell.

"I'll take this one," I said.

She accepted my coins, and I went to work slicing up Springsteen until he and the band formed a perfect head wrap. One way or another, the Boss was going for a ride. It was the least I could do for the roughneck Jersey prince of rock and roll.

YOU MAKE YOUR
OWN LUCK

I stood near the back of a cluttered little store in rural Ireland, sober and sound, but a little off-kilter and not entirely clear what to do with myself. My bicycle, like a trusted old dog, waited patiently out front. I could very easily have left my few selections on the closest shelf, slipped away and kept going, but I just had to stick around, if only to see what HE would do next.

The road makes the most timid among us reckless. Stay out long enough, beyond that emotional expiration date, and like it or not, you're going to have to fall back on luck and pray she receives you into her fickle embrace. And hope? Ask anyone who's lived for more than about fifteen minutes—they'll tell you something about that cagey bastard, far sketchier than luck.

Between countless hours of subpar television programing and long, sweaty waits in roped-off amusement park lines, I've had some serious time to get to know myself. This fueled a growing suspicion that I'm not built for hardcore survival. I'll do in a pinch; I might even acquit myself with some measure of verve and valor under rather specific circumstances—swerving the wheel to avoid a head-on, performing the Heimlich maneuver on someone gagging on a chicken bone, that sort of quick-thinking parlor trick. Moments in time that make good barroom tales later, but if we're talking about Discovery Channel drama—the speed of a gazelle, the bite of a cobra, the raw, primal, instinctive clawing, kicking and breaking-for-the-light level of survival over the long term—

It's not entirely my fault, though. I grew up near the mall.

Quit snickering. My guess is that you wouldn't fare much better. Collectively, we've become rather soft. Not a slight paunch around the evolutionary midsection either, but soft as in one of Pottery Barn's overstuffed couches you have to special-order out of a perfumey-smelling catalog. Aren't we the generation that invented reality TV? There we sit, playing with so many buttons on slick little keyboards or bemoaning the service at a certain trendy restaurant, then we count on clean machines and grimy attorneys to make it all better. Even subscribers perusing every damn word of *Men's Journal* and *Outside* magazine, taking the courses, memorizing whole chapters from *The Worst Case Scenario Survival Handbook,* going so far as to spend nights in little stuff sacks on exposed ledges—I hope they never have to find out if they're up for real survival. The best of us get by on grocery store food and dumb luck.

And that's fine, it's our lot in this day and age, but this bloke was packaging the stuff and selling it. Hawking it, actually, slipping a bit of luck in with a carton of smokes, toiletries, and ranch-flavored chips. I didn't know whether to tip my helmet at his entrepreneurial spirit or indict him for crimes against our waning sense of wonder in this world. HE turned out to be a rather charming chap named Randy.

Short, with the loose, rangy energy of a goalie. It's difficult to work up the appropriate level of indignant fervor for someone whose friends probably call him Handy Randy and buy him drinks just to hear some of his clever stories. But Randy's next move fanned my flames good. He didn't know I was in the store, peeking out from behind the canned fruit section like . . . well, like some sort of criminal, but Randy was the one pulling off a heist.

The two ladies he'd been helping, a pair of Dutch tourists fresh from kissing the Blarney Stone, had the un-fortunate luck—there's that word again—to stumble into this particular shop for some treats and a few provisions.

"Could it really be a four-leaf clover?" asked the sturdier of the two women, a bit of gray highlighting her long straight hair.

"That it is, ma'am. That it is indeed."

The ladies took care as they handed the ornate glass-and-wood case, about the size of a softcover book, back and forth.

He pretended to ignore them as the gals inspected the clover. It lay dead center on a lovely piece of crushed velvet, a deep and soothing purple color that was carefully chosen to accent the plant's symmetry and hue. Below the clover was an inscription, gold calligraphy on wood, something in Gaelic. Randy's timing was perfect. Just as they started to ask, he anticipated, "It's a wonderful old saying," followed by the slightest of pauses, then "May the road rise to meet you."

I could see the one holding the framed clover increase her grip around it. He finished them off with a very sweet closing statement. "Hard to put a price on something like that, it being the last one I've managed to locate this year.

Those are about as hard to find as ... well, four-leaf clovers."

They fell into laughter over his wit.

Randy gently removed it from her clutches and stared at the case as though he were gazing upon the portrait of a well-loved relative, gone now but not forgotten. I didn't hear how much they actually paid for it, but the purchase took several traveler's checks.

This was a fisherman of the highest order. The ink wasn't even dry on those checks when Randy stepped into the storeroom for only a moment or two. And I would love to tell you that he came back out with some canned goods or a few pints of milk for the front cooler, but a rather familiar case, with its snatch of purple crushed velvet catching the light, is all that appeared in his paws. The counterfeit clover found its spot by the register before the Dutch ladies had pulled away from the curb. Confidence to burn. It's a damn seductive quality. But his gifts were lost on me, for I'd seen behind the curtain.

As he rang up the last of my supplies I pointed at the frame. "These are pretty rare, eh?"

Randy raised an eyebrow, surprised at his own continued good luck. Some days the fish won't stop biting. A quick clearing of the man's throat before he twisted his neck, first to the left, then slowly back to the right—the sort of thing prizefighters do before going back into the ring.

"Rare as rain in the desert." He took in my bright blue rain jacket and damp bike gloves. "Or sunshine in Ireland," Randy added with a wink.

I stared at the framed clover, wondering if his shipment had been ordered by mail from that big clover plant in St.

Petersburg, Florida, where 40 percent of the world's four-leaf clovers are mass-produced like disposable razors or air fresheners, or whether it was simply a three-leaf variety altered by glue and dexterity. That would certainly cut down on shipping costs. Call me a cynic, but the ink from the Dutch gals' checks was still drying in the till. I'm no clover expert, but I grew up in Tampa and waited tables with a guy who had worked across the bay at the St. Pete plant for a spell. He said that science and marketing had taken all the luck, faith, and joy out of the shamrock story.

"You know how rare a four-leaf clover really is?" Randy asked me, rhetorically of course. He was deep in the zone where good salesmen find themselves on their best days.

I shook my head and leaned in.

"Less than one-tenth of one percent of clovers display a fourth leaf."

I offered a solemn "hmm."

"This isn't just an Irish belief, you know. Well before Christ hung from the nails, sun-worshiping Druid priests thought that if you possessed a four-leaf clover, you could spot witches and demons. And the Vikings wore the beloved clover into battle."

"And the inscription?" I asked.

He bit lightly on his top lip. "One for hope, a second for faith, a third for love, and may the final leaf of luck lead you home."

Handing him back the framed trinket, I nodded as if I were impressed. Then I pounced.

"I've always felt that I make my own luck."

He chuckled. "Do you now? Maybe you're confusing opportunities for luck. Common mistake. Luck's not something you manufacture. Just like a four-leaf clover, you have to stumble upon it . . . as you have today."

I took the frame back for another moment. His rangy energy abated a little. Feeling as if he'd set the hook deep, Randy was pausing before he reeled in the sale.

"You know what? I'm not sure I like the inscription on this one. Could you dig up another from the back room? That ditty about the road rising to meet you, the one you used to pinch a big score off those unsuspecting Dutch gals—that was perfect."

He stopped short, like a mime running into an imaginary wall. I put the frame back on the counter. My turn to wink. "I guess they didn't realize who puts the sham in shamrock."

Randy's confusion lasted about as long as his indignant stare, a few seconds. It was the look of someone who has been struck with a glancing blow and turns to lash back, only to realize it was an accident.

"Hey now, just keep your Alans on." He was chuckling. "Thing about you red-white-and-blue boys, you've had it good for so long, you don't think you need luck anymore. It's been relegated to cereal boxes and scratch-off lottery tickets over there, hasn't it? But everyone needs a nip or two of the clover's magic, even guys like you."

I'll say this, the man knew how to take a verbal punch. But damn it if there wasn't some vague, cotton-candy truth spinning around inside his words. I couldn't let it sway me from the topic, though, which was his blatant con.

Randy was playing the Yankee card, an easy hand. The problem, in his view, was a general cockiness based on my

country of origin: *Not your fault, really, just born that way*.
He probably equated it to having one arm shorter than the
other. I couldn't let his cheerful style and charm win me
over.

"Look, everyone has to make a living, but to hold the
tourists over a barrel using their memories of childhood
myths and a universal desire for a sure thing . . ." I took a
deep breath. "What you're doing here amounts to—well,
you're whoring the clover." Sometimes you know you're
being a self-righteous prick but you can't find the lever that
will shut your mouth fast enough. I figured my last dig,
completely uncalled for, would get me thrown out of his
store.

"It's the same reason I don't like places like Vegas," I
added for no apparent reason save that I wanted to deflect
some of my attack—that and I really don't like Vegas much.

Instead of tossing me out on my spandex-clad keester,
Randy closed the register and reached for his coat.

"You really don't like Vegas? Not even the fecking massive buffets or the brilliant floor shows I've heard so much
about?" He was taking the whore comment well.

"Okay, the buffets *are* extraordinary," I admitted. "You
ever been there? They have this place done up like a me-
dieval castle. The size of the turkey legs alone . . . Wait, I
wasn't finished with my diatribe."

Randy rolled out a three-speed bike from the stockroom. It appeared to be held together with rust and the
power of positive thinking.

"By all means. I just thought we'd be more comfortable
dismantling my character down at the pub. Unless you

don't want to share some crisps and the black stuff with a chancer like me?"

Damn it if his easy charm hadn't sucked me in when I was off thinking about that endless buffet table at the Excalibur.

In my defense, Randy traveled by bike, so I couldn't write him off as easily now. We pedaled along a quaint boreen into town. I learned that Randy was on his second marriage and had three children. While this put him under some financial hardship, he felt it had bloody well saved his life. "I did it all arseways until the day I married that gal."

He took a long look at my bike as we coasted down a slight hill to where I could see a cluster of streetlights and buildings.

"You say you've been nearly round the world without any major injuries?" He smiled. "I'd make the case that even if you don't believe in luck, she has your back, you tosser."

"Couldn't it just be fine motor skills, timing, and judgment keeping me in the game all these miles?"

Randy found me funnier than a Three Stooges festival. Only I was being serious.

"Truth is, Randy, I gave up all my rabbit's feet, Magic Eight Balls, and good-luck charms by high school. They're children's toys, dead weight on the bike or in my britches."

Britches? I was starting to affect the meter and playful colloquialisms of an Irishman and I'd been in the country for only a few weeks. I had to watch myself—there's nothing worse than a tourist trying to play native.

"You're bulletproof, then!" he mockingly confirmed.

"And I'm whoring the clover. The phrase has a gritty flavor to it. I'd put it on my business cards if I had any."

From the way Randy was riding, I had to assume his bicycle lacked brakes. He swerved and leaned to avoid obstacles and put his feet down when all else failed.

"But you're wrong about the power of believing in things," he added. "You have to think about luck, bad and good, as . . ." He bit his lip and gave it more thought. "As what happens when God has his back turned."

I'd give even money he'd used that line on countless tourists at the store counter, but still, it was damn good—poetic, even. We parked our bikes in front of the pub. I waited to see if Randy's boots were actually smoking from his Flintstones braking technique.

"Well, while the Almighty is looking the other way, do you mind if I tighten up your brakes?" I offered.

As I suspected, Randy was, along with being very lucky, a practical man. A few major adjustments to his levers, and the soles of his boots had a fighting chance of making it through the season.

It surprised me that for much of the time we talked about everything but the subject that had brought us together. For the record, Randy was as witty and charming as expected, more so after enough alcohol had lubricated my brain. He did not pontificate about the merits of the clover but asked instead about my travels and, as afternoon edged toward evening, confessed that he'd never had any real desire to leave his own little hamlet. Everyone knew Randy. Everyone loved Randy. I didn't remember seeing him pay for more than the first round, and I rode this wave of

Randy's popularity right up to the thin air of intoxication. But just when I thought the session was going to spin out of control, Randy announced that, sadly, we had to depart— family duties and all. He hoisted me up from the warm booth, and in the next moment we were standing in a steady rain. I followed Randy's lead, pulling huge snatches of fresh, damp evening air into the lungs in hopes that it might clear my head for riding.

"Well, I'm going to need more than a rabbit's foot to help me find a good spot to camp for the evening." I said this in a carefree tone that didn't match my situation: wet, homeless for the night, and slightly wobbly on my feet. It even sur-prised *me* that I wasn't more concerned about my welfare.

"Randy, I'm going to need some good directions."

"No, you won't. You can bed down on our couch tonight, if you'd like."

Moved by the offer, I felt compelled to point something out. "But I called you a clover whore."

"And after I let it sit for a while, I considered it a com-pliment."

I turned on my bike light and was about to ask Randy how far it was to his abode. But he'd already started rolling up the road. Another quick look down to find my pedals and my thoughts drifted to how bicycling in Ireland at dusk in a cool rain—as a romanticized traveler's adventure image—is far more pleasant as a daydream at, say, a dead-end McJob or in the comfort of your bed than as a firsthand experience. But what was I complaining about? A roof over my head for the night was only a short ride away, and I was in superb clover-whoring company. That's when I heard the crash. Sprinting my bike up the short incline, I crested the hill as fast as a Tour de France contender to find Randy sprawled across an all but deserted road.

My eyes darted around to see what had clipped him, but there was no traffic, cross streets, or any obstacles, really. He was either seriously hurt or simply lying there completely still to gather his thoughts. Without preamble Randy wobbled up and brushed himself off. He had acquired some good-sized scrapes along his right cheek and a load of gravel in his hair.

"What the hell happened?"

"Sometimes I'm denser than bottled shite, is what happened. I momentarily forgot my bike has brakes now. I'm grabbing the handlebars tight per usual, as I like to build up speed down the hill. Next thing I know I'm going arse over teakettle with the bike at a standstill behind me."

I checked his head, but it was devoid of holes and gaping wounds. He had sprung a leak through a torn spot at his elbow, though.

"You're bleeding."

"Just a scratch." He rubbed some spit across it, reasoning that the alcohol on his breath should serve as a disinfectant, then dabbed at it with the torn cloth of his shirt. "See, now that's a piece of luck. Nothing broken, the bike's okay, and we know the brakes work."

"There are easier ways to test these things," I said, feeling responsible to some degree.

"Just tell my wife it was a bike accident or she'll think I had a go with some wanker down at the pub. I owe a score or more to a fair number of those boys, and she's always mollycoddling me. Worried that my friends will turn one day and beat the quid right out of me. She worries too much. What she doesn't know is how I carry a pack of them on the store's books. I'd rather she worry I'll get beaten up than know I float them to payday and beyond."

"But you did wreck your bike, so we can just tell her the truth. Simple."

He spun the pedal to make sure the chain was still on. "You're not married yet, so I'll forgive that last comment. See, it's not like riding along from one thing to the next. This is it, lad. You have to pace yourself. Once you're together under one roof, the word *simple* disappears from the vocabulary."

When we reached Randy's door, Charlotte, his wife, asked right off who did this to him.

"The ground," I said before Randy could answer, shaking her hand as I entered their little place. "He took a spill on his bike."

Charlotte examined the injuries and seemed satisfied that they were indeed the result of gravity tussling with velocity and not a plonk's fist.

"I'm always saying it wouldn't kill you to get those brakes fixed." She swatted him gently with his own muddy cap before hanging it up for him. I flashed Randy a knowing smile. Fixing the brakes was what had gotten him in all this trouble.

Charlotte was young and quite stunning. It was almost as if they were playing house together, except that the children sitting in front of the tele looked quite permanent.

"Without brakes that bike's about as reliable as a chocolate teapot." She shook her head and stood back up before she could get comfortable around their petite kitchen table.

"Speaking of which, would either of you gentlemen care for a cup?"

I'd consumed enough tea during three weeks in Ireland that I could stand over a urinal and read my future.

"A cup sounds nice," I replied before I could put the brakes on myself.

I watched Randy play with his stepchildren. He offered them the boisterous roughhousing of a real dad. Charlotte and I talked over my adventures and her life in the not-so-big city as the tea cooled. Randy took the kids outside for a game of flashlight tag in the rain. After that it would be time for their baths.

"So how'd Randy get lucky enough to meet you?" I asked, complimenting her without, I hoped, coming off as too flirtatious.

She took a sip of her tea and shared that Randy had been married to her older sister; she'd wed a local man the summer after her sister married.

"We were bookend couples, always on one end of the other about town. Went to flicks, hung out at the pubs most nights until I had the twins and Meg. Colm and Randy were real mates. My sister, Glory, could be a real rusher. Never standing still long enough to give Randy kids, but he never begrudged her the career she was always planning to start. The holidays were coming up, and Glory insisted going all the way to Belfast for shopping." Charlotte looked outside for a moment. We could hear laughter coming from the backyard and see lights streaking through the window.

"Colm drove deliveries, so when Randy had to work the store and I couldn't find anyone to watch the young ones, Colm and Glory made the trip together to the city."

And I waited for her to close out this sordid family history with a Peyton Place ending. Now they're living on the peninsula, happy as clams in each other's arms while she and Randy pick up the pieces and try to raise a family off the dole. Something like that.

"They think the car bomb was meant for a reporter. Colm was double-parked right there when it went off. He always did that because he could get away with it in his delivery truck. Called it one of his few perks. Glory probably wanted to run into a shop for one more quick purchase."

"Jaysus." Without thinking I'd begun using the Irish way of stretching it out.

"From the looks of it, she was standing right between the car and the truck."

"I'm so sorry, Charlotte." What else could I say? She waved me off politely, either having made her peace with it or just not comfortable with pity in general.

"When we buried them, Randy said to me, 'It's not that people like you and me don't believe in love, it just doesn't believe in us.' "

Charlotte pushed a long strand of hair away from her face.

"Then a most unexpected thing happened. Randy moved in after the New Year. Step by bloody step we managed to come out of our nosedives, and when we found level ground again we were together. Only guilt keeps me from saying we're happier than ever. He dishes the kids everything that's left inside of himself at the end of the day. 'Course, we fight like alley cats when the urge strikes, but

Randy clearly misspoke when he said love had given up on this lot."

I smiled at her, washed my cup in the sink, grabbed my rain jacket, and in no time found myself zigzagging through wet grass, dodging beams of lights with a very lucky man and his three little clovers.

People will often ask if the bike slows me down too much to get all I can out of my travels. Well, I've hoofed it and gone by rail, rented cars, and reluctantly let those winged metal tubes transport me over oceans and across continents, but two-wheel tramping always lets me set the perfect tempo.

Over breakfast the next morning I told Randy I'd changed my mind, maybe not about luck but I was willing to hedge my bets now. Did he have any of his framed four-leaf clover stock there at the house? I wanted to give him the first sale of the day. After the time I'd had with him, the trinket begged to be bought as a conversation piece alone.

Randy eased back and winked. "Like I said before, that one over at the store is the last I have. Furthermore, I'm not sure I want to sell it to someone who just yesterday didn't believe he needed it." Randy scooped up his last bite of eggs and had a good chuckle.

I knew he'd part with the item in question. Now it was only a matter of how high I was willing to go for a keepsake of our time together.

Reading my mind, he added, "It's gonna cost you. The clover whore is feeling rather wicked today."

As we readied ourselves to ride over to the store to-gether, I cornered his stepdaughter, Meg, and asked if Randy ever took them on four-leaf-clover scavenger hunts. "This summer we're all supposed to caravan to the best spot on the isles for them. He says it's his secret field."

Was she in on the con with him, or did Randy really . . . ? And did it matter? Maybe I could, this one time, just leave it as one of life's little mysteries. In the end I re-sisted walking through the stockroom door for the definitive answer. Instead I broke out some precious traveler's checks. But Randy wanted to give it to me for nothing, as if he'd won the standoff and that was all that mattered. Like a couple of old Jewish ladies trading advice, we went back and forth until I said he should buy some presents for the kids with the funds. That worked for him. And remembering them on the grass, all slickers, flashlights, and laughter, I was certain he'd do it as long as the debts down at the pub didn't come calling.

This might come as something of a surprise, but I can't read Gaelic and I kept forgetting to show my little keepsake to people who could. So when I arrived back in the States I had no idea what the inscription really said. Somehow it's more fun that way. If anyone asks, I tell them:

> **LUCK'S WHAT HAPPENS WHEN**
> **GOD HAS HIS BACK TURNED.**

Cheers, Randy.

THREE
(UNLIKELY)
AMIGOS

We stood together in the dead center of Australia, an unholy trinity of touring cyclists gazing across a continent from atop the monolith of Ayers Rock. Rowdy Alabama Shane on the left, yours truly the Metal Cowboy on the right, and young Norbu, all five glorious feet of him—a man whom I'd come to think of as the Horizontal Sherpa, balancing proud and steady—bookended between us.

When we began chewing up miles together a few hours outside the capital city of Canberra, you'd have taken some damn long odds—retire-on-the-winnings-size odds, in fact— that we wouldn't still be pedaling as a trio and sharing this perch more than a thousand miles down the road. Small differences had become magnified over the miles, riding styles had taken a toll, and circumstances—in this case a wicked bartender named Connie—had conspired to break us apart. But fierce weather, the steel-belt-thick bond of road warriors forged on bikes in the middle of nowhere, and a broken chain linked us back together.

"Well, boys, that wasn't nothing but a little bitty hike, if you ask me." Alabama Shane was in the habit of call-ing everyone "boys" and sharing his thoughts on most subjects well before he'd been asked. A retired telephone line installer, Shane claimed to be brushing up against the long hairs of seventy but resembled a man twenty years younger. He was the type who rose every morning ready to roll no matter what havoc the previous day had presented.

Maybe laughter is the fountain of youth. Shane could sure turn a phrase, dance a bastardized cross between a jig and the hustle, and keep himself and those around him in stitches from the moment he rolled out of his tent in the morning until he conveniently ran out of steam just around the after-dinner dishwashing hour. Norbu didn't always get the rowdy southerner's regional references, and that thick drawl gummed up the transmission for everyone now and then. Even so, Alabama Shane could make the Sherpa double over with laughter and cause a spontaneous combustion of food to spew from his mouth. After this happened the first time, I chose to plant my behind beside my Nepalese friend rather than across the campfire from him, at least during mealtimes.

"But it is a helluva view, gents," Shane added. When he wasn't calling us boys, we were gents.

Norbu grunted in agreement and we stared silently from the majestic summit. After weeks of cycling the dusty reaches of the Stuart Highway together, Norbu had learned to conserve his conversational energy around Alabama Shane. He did this by issuing a deep-throated grunt if he agreed and a high-pitched one if he dissented. Norbu was actually a ball of energy and could carry the conversational baton rather well. His English, like the three other languages he spoke, had been perfected while toting gear up mountains for rich American, Japanese, and European thrill seekers, but aside from the fact that Alabama Shane could wear anyone's ear down to a smooth useless nub, Norbu was most at ease when directing his compact power into actions. Some mornings I'd realize he had our tents down and stowed before I'd brewed the first pot of tea and before Shane had opened up his endless can of "You know you're a redneck if . . ." jokes. And while he opted for the unorthodox and orthopedically risky practice of wearing his gear on his back rather than in panniers attached to the bike, Norbu kept up nicely, leading the pace line for many miles at a time.

Ayers Rock is a hulking red clay oddity in the shape of an overturned coffee cup, the primitive variety that a second-grader might sculpt for his or her mother in art class, minus the handle. Nothing but desert floor surrounds this Australian monolith—officially the largest one on earth (no offense to Stanley Kubrick)—giving it center stage on the horizon.

"I'm headed for that big red rock in the desert. The one that changes all those colors at sunrise and sunset and the Abos worship like there's no tomorrow." Alabama Shane announced this at our first meeting. We'd discovered a comfortable pedaling cadence right away and had settled into a conversation.

Ayers Rock does indeed appear to be different shades of red depending upon the time of day. It's a fiery burst of red at sunrise, nearly brown by midday, navel-orange-colored around sunset, and a burnt maroon at dusk. But the way Shane referred to it, you might think the rock went from teal to canary yellow, then on to a kelly green—sort of in Fourth of July fireworks mode—as people stood around marveling at it. Shane might not exactly be a Mensa member, but I'd soon discover that he had easygoing charm and plenty of laid-back street smarts.

"You mean Ayers Rock?"

"That's the one," Shane confirmed. "Damn, why can't I remember a name like that? Problem is, it sounds too much like a beer I drank with abandon on summer evenings after working the meat counter of the Piggly Wiggly. Miracle I didn't cut off a thumb or a pinky, as hung over as I felt some days. Anyhow, I suspect that's the source of my mental blockage. Besides, they keep telling me I'm crazy to want to ride this bike all the way out there when a perfectly reliable tour bus makes the run a couple times a day."

And that's when our friendship officially began. We smiled and nodded almost in unison because we owned an answer to one of the best riddles on earth—one, it seems, only a minority manage to untangle each generation.

"But if you have to explain why you want to ride a bicycle, then—" I started to say.

"Then you should just save your breath, 'cause they ain't gonna get it in a million damn years." Shane liked to finish other people's sentences. He did it with such flourish and bravado, though, that much of the time it felt like he was simply confirming your own intelligence, even when it wasn't exactly what you'd been planning to say.

"Where you headed?" he asked between gulps from his water bottle. It appeared he was drinking, no kidding, sweet tea, just the way it's served in the deep South. I grew up in Florida and can recognize a jar of sweet tea anywhere.

At the time, I'd been debating whether to head north to Alice Springs—Alabama Shane's announced route—or make a right turn just beyond Adelaide and barrel into the no-man's-land of the Nullabor Plain, the outback of the outback. Either way we had six hundred miles of shared pavement together if we wanted the company.

A ride to the Red Center (what the tourism board cleverly calls Ayers Rock, since it's at the geographic midpoint of the continent) meant backtracking some four hundred miles once I'd had my fill of the famous boulder. There was always the bus ride option. I don't consider it cheating mileage or the spirit of a bike tour if I've already covered the ground once. It was more the thought of enduring a long bus trip that had me flinching. I'd sworn off bus rides like some people shake off drug addiction.

Shane capped his tea and shifted gears for the small hill we were approaching.

"I pinch myself each morning just to make sure I'm not dreamin' up this Aussie adventure in a hospital bed somewhere." Alabama Shane said this with a faraway gaze and a grin that even poorly done bridgework couldn't mar. "Life's something you can't pigeonhole or predict no matter how much you try. It's a kick, really, that I got the chance at all. Honest, now, tell me this isn't some beautiful hallucination I'm sweating through at the clinic. I'm really on my bike in Oz, aren't I?"

In that moment, Shane shed maybe sixty of his years right before my eyes. He morphed into an overgrown boy on a bike taking his victory lap for all those seasons he'd kept his head down and his chin up and gone off to work, the years and hard living carving away at his focus and strength. Surely he pondered things over and calculated odds for such things as "Will I get my flight of fancy before the big fade or cardiac clutch arrives uninvited?" Springsteen once sang that in the end, what you don't surrender the world strips away. That being the case, rowdy Alabama Shane's tenacity touched me.

I heard myself saying, "Hey, just happens I'm headed to Ayers Rock also." And decided it had a nice ring. "By the way, the Aboriginal name for that famous magnetic mound is Uluru." (Pronounced oolooroo.)

Alabama Shane spit some tea through a slight gap between his front teeth. "Can't say I ever drank beer named anything close to that." He thought it over. "You got any other names for the rock? 'Cause it sounded like you were in some pain, maybe even pulled a muscle just tryin' to sound out that one."

And there it was. Alabama Shane had discovered a linguistic weak spot, my Achilles' heel: the fluid pronunciation of foreign languages. Seeing as my mother speaks four languages, taught French and Spanish in the school system, and impresses people to this day with her perfect accents and natural abilities, I hang my head in shame each time I struggle through asking for directions in Mexico or verbally maul an order from a menu in a French restaurant. It's not that my mother neglected our education. Just the opposite—we were issued copies of *War and Peace* while still in diapers. But we came up during the height of America as a superpower, those arrogant decades when strip malls rose out of the dirt like boils on the retail landscape and, like a national tidal wave, a collective planning for the country's bicentennial celebrations washed over our thoughts. If we'd been out wandering the streets chatting in Spanish or French . . . well, my mom must have rationalized that childhood can be painful enough without socially handicapping your kids in such a political climate.

"Uluru." I said it again, louder but still with hesitation.

Shane smiled. "Now turn your head and cough, 'cause I'm sure you gave yourself a hernia that time."

The third unlikely amigo joined our rolling laughfest shortly after breakfast the next morning.

"We've got company," Alabama Shane announced. "I think it's an Aboriginal on a bicycle." Heat waves were already dancing on the far-off blacktop, making it hard to get a real bead on the man, but he could have been Aboriginal, or even a polar bear on a bike at that distance. We waited. The figure on the horizon grew larger and came into focus as I studied some confusing signage painted on a post at that lonely intersection and Alabama Shane went into an elaborate process of shaking up his tea. Shane would agitate his beverage like a washing machine on heavy rinse until he deemed it the right consistency for his discerning taste buds.

When Norbu rolled to a stop we saw that he was riding a Scott Fisher, a bike with no place for traditional panniers. He turned out to be Nepalese, not Aboriginal, and was also on his way to Ayers Rock. At twenty years old, Norbu was a veteran mountaineer and professional Sherpa. We made introductions and fell into a pace line. No one spoke or stopped pedaling for the better part of two hours. Riding behind Norbu, I noticed the tight, stringy calf muscles of someone who hadn't stood still for more than fifteen minutes during his life. My guess? He didn't have cable TV or own an easy chair.

A lonely truck stop appeared on the horizon, and we made for it, resting together under a tattered awning.

"The big red rock"—this was what Alabama Shane had taken to calling it—"should be a cakewalk for you, Mr. Norbu. Seeing as you hike up the sides of Mount Everest and the like every day of the week."

"It's just Norbu," he said. "And yes, it will be quite easy because I have no intention of climbing it."

I looked over at Shane, and he offered a search-me shrug.

"This ain't your way of telling us you're really afraid of heights or something?"

Norbu gave Shane a disarming smile. "Not afraid, no, just tired of all the climbing. I don't care if I ever reach another summit."

Shane nodded. "Job burnout. I know it well. Came back from Disney World with the family one vacation and had to holler and yell just to force my butt back up the first telephone pole. Nothin' pretty 'bout a grown man standing beside morning rush-hour traffic, screamin' at himself. Scared some of the commuters, I did."

When I couldn't add anything to this bonding session, Shane took up my slack. "Don't mind old Joe over there. He's one of those rare bastards who does what he wants and people hand over the loot anyway." Shane had everything pegged right except for the old part and, I'm fairly certain, the bastard part. But I do wander the earth under a rather lucky star. This cantankerous waiter I once worked with was fond of saying, "It's never too late for your life to go south on you, remember that." Fair enough, but should you live it uninspired just so you don't have very far to fall? That's a dinner tray of twisted logic.

A snapshot of the three of us at that moment, bags and bikes shining in the sun and bodies climbing triumphantly back into the saddle, just might have invigorated others to pursue a life less ordinary, a road less traveled—that or force them to sleep with the lights on for the next few weeks. We weren't in any danger of taking top honors in the best-dressed category. And was that me or Shane who smelled like German cheese rolled inside dirty laundry?

"It's hard to burn out from a job you never liked. I think I enjoyed climbing for about one afternoon when I was a child, but now it is the same for me as a person working in a factory. They tell me, 'But Norbu, it is so beautiful.' I say, 'Then you climb.' I want to ride my bike over the next hill, see other places of beauty, and not have to watch my feet pass through the clouds one more time. Mountains are supposed to be holy places, not high-altitude prisons."

One of the clients had brought a bike to Nepal but decided to leave it at base camp rather than ship it home. Norbu claimed the rig and learned to ride, and once he had some money saved, he walked down the mountain for what he swore was the last time.

"When my resources run low I will work at any job along the way—any, that is, but carrying packs into the high country."

I offered that I'd do anything but wait tables again beside guys who smelled like death and cheap aftershave.

"I'll do anything," Shane said. We thought there might be a caveat, but that was it. "It's easy for me to say, though, 'cause I'm carrying a bunch of credit cards."

By Adelaide we'd become, if not blood brothers, then honest-to-goodness amigos on a mission. It was our first night together under an actual roof. There's a certain festive atmosphere brought on by full-body bathing and a set of clean clothes. It put rowdy Alabama Shane in a magnanimous frame of mind. He offered to take us out to dinner. Being cyclists, fiscally limited by anyone's accounting methods, we couldn't turn down a free meal. It felt strange to me to walk beside these men minus our armada of props: gloves, helmets, and water bottles. And to look at one another shaved and devoid of road dust? Well, now, that was like being introduced to a distant relative of the mutts I'd been pedaling next to all these days. We wandered around hungry for many blocks before stumbling upon a little restaurant, no sign but some of the best Egyptian cuisine I've ever tasted. With a wicked glint in his eye and the flaky remnants of dessert on his chin, Shane announced that the belly dancing show and lessons were about to begin.

"And you can't back out 'cause it's nonrefundable, boys."

This was our first exposure to Shane's jig/hustle dance number. I wondered how many doses of this medicine, like radiation treatments, might kill a man. Norbu asked aloud if we needed shots to protect ourselves. This caused me to laugh so hard, I resembled a cat choking on a hairball.

Norbu was a natural. All he lacked was a belt of coins and a veil of sheer fabric to turn pro. I thought I was representing myself admirably until Shane hollered out, "I've seen a corpse move more than that, JoJo. Put your hips into it, for pity's sake. You dance like a PTA mother."

Shane demonstrated, but all I saw was a man jerking about like he had an inner-ear infection. I turned to the instructor, but she came off so seductive that I forgot what I was doing there and stood still and appreciative in the middle of the room until I embarrassed her. Norbu turned out to be my saving grace. There's nothing repulsive or even sexual about a demure Sherpa executing belly-dance moves in Adelaide.

———

A dust storm caught us outside of nowhere along the Stuart Highway as if we were standing still. It was the leisurely downside of a scorcher afternoon, the time of day when the miles have hypnotized you to a point where you still see the road in front of you but don't take it in on a conscious level. It's more about pedaling on instinct and the promise of dinner in the near future. Shane, a few hundred yards behind us, was the first to notice a wall of red dust and debris bearing down fast and unrelenting. It reached too far in either direction for us to scramble off the road and hope to skirt around its edges.

"Boys, you try to outrun it. Maybe she'll change course or die down." These were Shane's orders, barked and spat across the distance as though from a marine who knows he's doomed but is attempting, as a final heroic act, to get some of his platoon out alive. It might sound melodramatic in retrospect, but at that moment, glancing over my shoulder to witness a rolling curtain of grit engulf Shane, I had no idea whether this would pass harmlessly or end in utter tragedy. I cranked my pedals as if the devil himself were riding hot and heavy on my rear rack.

Note to self: If the wind wants to catch you, there's

nothing you can muster to outpace it. It would win the Tour de France without even breaking a sweat. I felt this breath of heated air rush against my back and kiss me forward. It was so sure and gentle at first that it could have been the hand of a parent giving that extra measure of velocity when a child first learns to ride without training wheels. For a instant I was filled with the false hope that this push was all I needed to stay in front of our rocky red demon. Then the sky went dim. Dust, stones, sticks, and worse whistled and clattered over me, filling the open spaces of my helmet. I spotted a T-shirt that had been loosely attached to my back rack fly by and disappear into oblivion. Visibility went from a few feet to inches and then to nothing beyond the tip of my helmet.

Stopping was inevitable, but that would risk a major collision with Norbu, who'd been in a full sprint the last time I'd glanced back. My instincts forced my hands to the brakes. I veered to the right and hoped Norbu was still on his earlier course. When he didn't slam into me seconds later, I stumbled off the bike and hunched down in the most protected area I could find—the space between the pedals and the rear bags.

I know it didn't last more than a few minutes, but at the time I had no idea how long I remained crouched and covered. When I did chance unfolding, in night-flowering plant fashion, I thought I'd be staring over a scene from an Allstate insurance commercial. Instead, there was no hint of the menacing force that had blown through moments earlier. Norbu had stopped a few yards behind me. He'd tucked himself over his bike handlebars, looked ahead and used the backpack he wore to protect himself from the brunt of it. I couldn't find Shane for a moment and feared the worst. Rather than a wicked witch riding her bike inside the tornado, I flashed on an image of Shane chasing a swirling jar of sweetened tea at the mouth of a windstorm for all of eternity. You can imagine how I was thrown, then, when I discovered him fifty yards *ahead* of us facing the wrong direction. Shane displayed countless pinprick-size cuts on his arms, his legs, and the back of his neck. Apparently he had decided to ride blindly through it, accomplishing the impressive feat of remaining on his bike. But at a cost.

"I got a little turned around there at the end. I think I pedaled back into the face of it."

"Jesus," I said with subdued reverence.

"These? Hell, I've had mosquito bites worse than this."

Clearly shaken, Norbu commented, "Something hit my pack hard. I think maybe a boulder?"

"Let's go find us a drink," said Shane, the comment betraying his casual bravado and exposing the impact this episode had inflicted upon him.

Norbu grunted in the affirmative pitch.

My legs were still shaking, flushed and pulsing with adrenaline. I cranked over the pedals and tried to steady myself. This wasn't promising, considering that the closest bar could be hours away.

"What's your favorite drink?" I asked Shane, thinking that the query would be good for a lengthy discussion—sure to distract me from my shaky frame of mind and wobbly body.

"All of them," he said with uncharacteristic brevity. "I did tell you boys I'm an alcoholic, right?"

We waited for the punch line. We'd still be waiting if

Norbu hadn't offered another solemn grunt and set a blistering pace into the setting sun. With or without the jab, I knew Shane was kidding . . . he was always kidding.

There was really no telling where we were. No markers or signs of any kind, not even a trail of bread crumbs. If asked, I'd have said we were somewhere along the Stuart Highway, Australia, planet Earth, end of story. We weren't exactly a walking advertisement for the global positioning system. Nobody had even consulted a map in days. I liked to joke that dingos had eaten my maps at the border.

But a few miles down we heard music coming from inside a little building and saw a beer sign in its one grimy window. This seemed quite enough for three dusty, wrung-out amigos.

"Amaretto sours, 'cept I renamed them Amarillo sours on account of how many I downed with good ol' boys from Texas," Shane said. He was answering my favorite drink question from a few hours before. Our third round of beers must have jogged something in his memory. Not having a favorite drink per se, unless Dr Pepper counted, I nodded, letting Norbu field the discussion. I decided to have a closer look around. This took all of thirty seconds. The bar, while not an exact replica of a backyard clubhouse we'd enthusiastically drawn up blueprints for in fifth grade, came damn close. It was cluttered and dark and there were dogs panting on the cement floors that you had to step over if you wanted to get anywhere. But where did you need to go? It had been erected, I'm quite sure, with throwaway materials from construction sites blown in on the wind and salvaged equipment not burned beyond recognition during insurance fires.

Its inhabitants were made up largely of those relatives most likely to cause loud, awkward scenes at weddings by French-kissing the bride, stumbling into the cake, or passing out with the microphone still gripped in one hand after performing an ABBA tune in the buff.

Three amigos drinking in bike clothing didn't raise an eyebrow.

In fact, we fit in so nicely that before long half the bar was listening to the tale of our windstorm scare. They cheered as Shane showed off his battle scars. He stood on a chair and modeled the countless cuts, then mooned the group for good measure. The place roared, and I felt the best I had all day.

A while later Connie, the grandmotherly barkeep, informed me, "I think you should go check on your friend. He's getting belligerent with the wrong pack of wolves over there."

When I located the always generous, good-natured Alabama Shane, he was well on his way to an Aussie ass kicking. It took me longer than it should have to realize this wasn't another of Shane's practical jokes or pieces of redneck performance art. It had to do with a drinking game and several rounds he didn't think he should have to buy for three rather upset gentlemen. I tried to purchase the scabby mates some tranquillity, but this went beyond beer money to some choice statements Shane had made about their sexual habits—a no-no on any continent.

"Could you cut him some slack? He doesn't look it, but this man's a senior citizen. Show them your AARP card, Shane."

What would have brought a chuckle to my pal's lips on any other occasion turned his anger in my direction.

"I don't need you trying to save me, JoJo. I've been raised already. One mother was enough." Then he pushed me away and marched over to the bar. The angry Aussies said they'd take care of Shane when he stepped out of the place, and if I got in the way, I'd be collateral damage.

And here I'd thought we'd weathered the storm.

Connie, kind but still an independent woman of business, kept pouring Shane drinks even after I discreetly asked her to cut him off.

"This is a bar, honey." She had a point.

The only person I could turn to was Norbu.

"He wasn't kidding when he said he was an alcoholic," Norbu mused.

"If you knew this, why'd we come in here?"

Norbu said he hadn't been sure before, but now, well . . . Regardless, he didn't think anything could be done. "This happens a lot in climbing. When they want to beat the mountain, they're going to do it with or without you. You shoulder some of the burden, lighten the load, but if they want to kill themselves to stand on top, then trying to stop them only makes it worse."

I didn't see how I could make getting beaten to death in the desert worse. Nonetheless, we informed Shane we'd set up camp a few miles down the highway on the right side of the blacktop.

"Run along, boys. I think I'm going to get lucky with ol' Connie here."

I felt sick about the whole thing—not the thought of two

elderly folks harmlessly rubbing their body parts together, but that we were abandoning Shane in a tight spot when he was not at the top of his game.

Norbu was more hopeful. "He's been an alcoholic for this long, he must be pretty good at it."

The angry Aussies were not outside when we saddled up. I made one more halfhearted pitch to Norbu. "Let's just go back in and hustle him out."

He grunted no and we spun into the darkness.

Three days later Shane was still AWOL somewhere in Oz. We were hundreds of miles north of that bar, and I decided I had to let it go. Either the flying monkeys had grabbed him or Shane was pedaling along the red brick road behind us, soothing the last of a killer headache with some sweet tea.

"You want to play?" Norbu was spreading out Shane's beloved dominoes across his sleeping bag. "Shane gave them to me back in Adelaide." Gloom descended again. I kept thinking of him in the past tense.

Later we decided that a grit-clogged chunk of links in Norbu's chain had to be removed or the thing was going to keep falling off all the way Ayers Rock. We'd ignored the problem as long as possible. Link removal is delicate work. Even with the right tool, if you push the post too far and it falls out, you will spend the better part of an afternoon trying to get it back in place. Thing is, I'm the guy to call if you need a car demolished with a sledgehammer or fish loaded off a truck—not detail work. Norbu appeared to be cut from the same cloth. We huddled over the chain for the better part of an hour, cursing and sweating as we tried to turn it into something resembling useful equipment. When a truck pulled over, we gave it little notice. People, God love 'em, were always stopping to see if we needed a ride somewhere, as if pedaling these devices was a form of punishment and they were the governor sent there to commute our sentences.

Rowdy Alabama Shane unloaded his bike and gear from the back of the truck. He looked fine if not exactly fit for a dead man.

We stood around not talking for a long, painful minute or two. Of course it was the Alabama Slamma who finally broke this levee of silence.

"Chain troubles, boys?"

I held up the tool.

"If you fix chains like you belly-dance, JoJo, we'll be here till sunup tomorrow."

I handed Shane the equipment.

"Did you get lucky with Connie?" Norbu asked.

Shane let go of a deep breath. "Turns out nobody gets lucky with Connie."

We watched steady hands that had stripped miles and miles of telephone line fix the post in place on their first try. Shane was still on the ground when he said, "I wanna thank you gents for not pointing out what a shitheel I was the other night."

"The day's still young," I noted.

He closed his eyes and smiled. "You know, I read that it's supposed to be a privilege to participate in your own decay. Thing is, I feel a little overprivileged sometimes."

Norbu nodded.

I rocked back on my heels. "I didn't know you could read."

And like that we were amigos again, stumbling blindly back onto the red brick road, rolling toward a rock that one of us couldn't name and another refused to climb. Me, I still had little idea what was drawing my wheels to it in the first place, beyond the brochures and this vague need for a destination.

This lack of focus was nothing new.

My sixth-grade teacher, a stone-cold mercenary who channeled the ghost of Mussolini every time the bell rang, wrote a note across the comment portion of an otherwise glowing report card: "Joe has unlimited potential, but he lacks focus." I took this to mean that the school system had not broken my spirit yet. When she fell ill, we covered a large get-well card with little sayings. Some of the students drew flowers and yearbook-style smiley faces. I used the opportunity to dash off this: "Focusing on only one thing can limit your potential." My smug glow of superiority dimmed somewhat when we learned she'd actually had a nervous breakdown and attempted to make her trains stop permanently with a bottle of sleeping pills. While this disturbed me greatly, it also helped strengthened the notion that wandering around aimlessly from time to time holds value—even more so when done in good company.

━ ■ ■ ━

"Well, I just promised Shane I'd climb that bloody rock," Norbu told me while we scrubbed the dinner pots with dirt and gravel, rinsing them with a pinch of precious water.

"And he promised not to drink anything stronger than tea from now on."

"Do you believe him?"

Norbu smiled. "Do you believe me?"

"Boys, finish those up later. I got the dominoes out, and I just remembered some other redneck jokes."

The company was anything but boring.

———

We camped at Yulara, a dusty red stone's throw from Ayers Rock. With its modern, almost cushy amenities, we were feeling a bit spoiled. I giggled like a schoolgirl when my caboose came to rest on a real toilet seat with a door on the stall. A door, for mercy's sake—what would they think of next? Norbu spoke of the shower as a religious experience. We'd become tolerant if not immune to windstorms, rain, rockslides, washed-out roads, blackflies, and skin-shredding heat, all the while simply pulling over to patches of flat ground, kicking away the rocks, and calling it home for the night.

Kata Tjuta National Park is owned and run by the Aborigines. The government handed the land back to them some years before, so this attraction did not come with a Disney World–style marketing package attached to it. You were free to experience the ancient caves covered in Aboriginal paintings, eroded rock faces, and freakish formations without some perky park "cast member" dressed in a Dreamtime Crow or Lizard outfit filtering and dolling up the natural beauty that needs no explanation or script.

Our first day in the park was spent back on the bikes. We pedaled around the circumference road, stopping to hike into caves that caught our fancy and to check out the plants and animals around the base of this massive mound.

"Damn, it says here that two-thirds of the rock lies beneath the surface." Shane had a way of marveling at small wonders and big ones alike, but this time his enthusiasm matched the subject matter. We stared at Ayers Rock. "It's like a big red boil, isn't it?" He also had a knack for trashing a reverent moment.

"It's more like the top of an iceberg," Norbu countered.

"Hell, when did you ever see an iceberg that was red and—"

I wandered off. Sometimes a man just needs the blessing of his own company.

Well before sunrise we woke to make the climb. Not because it was an epic ascent; rather, because it's uncomfortably hot and often windy by late morning and on into the middle of the day atop the big red rock.

I was struck with a brilliant idea. We would carry a bicycle with us to the summit, then take pictures of ourselves holding it up, king of all creation, top of the world, momma, a triumphant trio captured on Kodachrome for all time.

Three unstoppable amigos.

Park officials informed me that only small backpacks and gear were allowed, their fear being that cyclists would try to ride down the slippery surfaces of the mound, turning a sacred site into a dangerous extreme-sport playground.

"You don't understand—the bicycle *is* sacred to me," I explained. "It's one of the most tangible pieces of evidence I have for the existence of God—it and cantaloupe, of course." This drew even more looks of concern from management. Hey, they might believe in Dreamtime, singing the universe into creation, and whatnot, but I was mouthing what sounded like serious woo-woo gibberish. Norbu and Shane understood my point but, also being zealots to the cycling cause, carried no weight with the rangers. A blind man could spot this as a lost cause. Somewhere our names were being placed on a watch list. I stopped before we were barred from the park altogether.

We settled for hoisting up our bike helmets and pumps in a victory salute.

———

Norbu eyed the long path leading to the summit but did not step forward.

Shane and I waited.

"Would it help if one of us carried your pack?" Shane offered. The Alabama Slamma was full of surprises—insight, irony, and poetic justice, whether he was fully aware of it or not.

Satisfaction oozing from every pore, Norbu extended his load to Shane, who immediately handed it over to me.

"JoJo?"

I smiled, incredulous. "I guess that means I will be your Sherpa today. Mind I don't fall too far behind, or you'll have to dock my pay."

At the summit we waited until a friendly couple had a good look around before asking them to snap our photo. Lots of shuffling through bags and hunting inside zipped pouches followed, but between the three of us we'd managed to leave all of our cameras and film back at the secure area in the youth hostel.

The couple offered to take a shot with their own camera and send us a copy. Somewhere in Australia there's a family vacation album that sports a conversation-stopping picture of three mangy amigos waving bike helmets and tire pumps like madmen atop a big red rock . . . wandering souls who, against some hefty odds, were having the time of their lives.

I'd pay good money for that picture now.

ALMOST NAKED
LUNCH

Lunch is a simple affair. Nothing to get worked up about. That's why Norbu, Alabama Shane, and I were so quick to pounce on our newfound cycling pal's offer of a midday snack out at the colony. We being the three unlikely amigos who had pedaled our way to the Red Center of Australia. Norbu, a former professional Sherpa of the Everest variety who now despised climbing anything taller than a high chair, Alabama Shane, a retired telephone line repairman who we'd let climb anything but back into the bottle, and myself, a rather sunbaked Metal Cowboy who long ago climbed onto the saddle of a bike and seemed to have forgotten how to climb back off.

Our newest wheel man, hugging the end of the pack, introduced himself as Digger. A tanned and rather spirited Aussie (but then I have met very few who weren't—spirited, that is), he set a nice cadence for a day rider and added much-needed energy to our push that morning. We learned that Digger's nickname came from his prowess on the volleyball court. He was certain that his friends out at the colony would find our stories a hoot, and we were equally sure we'd find their food top-flight. Free and filling are attractive come-ons to a touring rider.

Everything has its price, though.

"Did you see it? I swear that man by the gate was stark raving naked," Alabama Shane hollered as we spun into the summer camp setting of Digger's retreat. It was quite a spread. We were near the coast, where everything is lush greens and Technicolor clear blues.

"What?" I said. Having been involved in a fierce wrestling match with my water bottle, I'd missed Shane's alleged naked-man sighting. That I'd been spared a look at this particular Aussie wildlife was not a problem to me.

"Sans clothing," Norbu volunteered. Ah, Norbu, a master of understatement.

Digger waved us over to a good spot to park our bikes. His was a kind face and he'd acted quite lucid up to that point, but Digger now appeared to be taking off far too much of his gear, like his pants. I know my face registered concern, but it was Alabama Shane who crystallized our thoughts aloud.

"What in hell's going on here?"

Digger appeared confused, but this did not stop the man from tucking his shorts and bike shoes inside his pannier, rendering him now completely nude. Judging from Digger's even, all-over tan, this was not the one-time act of a gentleman suffering the advanced stages of sunstroke or dehydration.

"When I said this was a naturalist's retreat center, a nudist colony, you guys seemed thrilled. I would not have extended the invitation if it was going to make anyone uncomfortable."

A simple rule to follow: When riding bikes in a pace line with a slight headwind, words do get garbled from back to front, and pass by completely unheard at times from front to back. All I remembered was "nature colony," as in a Mutual of Omaha Down Under—cuddly koalas eating fruit in the high branches.

"I thought you were talking about some sort of art colony," Shane volunteered.

Meanwhile, Norbu had shed his clothing with such speed that one could only conclude the outfit had just been exposed to high levels of radiation. I took one look at our Nepalese friend, shook my head at this novel turn of events, and began to strip off my own clothes.

Alabama Shane assessed the situation while drawing a long pull from his jar of sweet tea. He spit a dash of it through the slight gap in his teeth for emphasis, then dismounted and disrobed.

"Momma always said my body was nothin' to be ashamed 'bout. But my old lady's been refuting said wisdom for going on thirty years now."

Lord, if this be part of your master plan, give me strength, I thought, *because I'm about to experience the unplugged, bootleg version of the Alabama Slamma.*

We stood around for a moment, like boys in a gym shower without the shower, trying to meet each other's gazes at eye level as much as possible.

It was Digger who ended our summit meeting of idiots. "It's a clothing-optional colony, by the way. Nudity's not mandatory."

This guy was just a wealth of surprises and always one step ahead of us with them. A bloomin' Willie Wonka Down Under. By then we'd already shed our clothing, if not our inhibitions, hadn't we? No one in our trio appeared man enough to admit his embarrassment and get dressed. In a moment of unpremeditated genius I grabbed for my bike helmet. When I glanced over at Shane all he had for coverage was his jar of sweet tea. Norbu carried nothing but his pride as we walked through the lodge. Some guys are lucky like that.

When we stepped into the courtyard nearly three decades seemed to peel away. Jerry Garcia was still alive; the world's most annoying gadget, the cell phone, had yet to be invented; and nudity ruled the day. But not a Bob Guccione portrait of undress; this was more of an earth-mother-meets-happy-children-playing-on-the-Slip-'N-Slide-in-the-backyard style of nakedness.

I observed folks playing a game of horseshoes in the buff living in harmony with nude people practicing tai chi. Several folks stood poised on either side of a volleyball net, but God love 'em, they had the originality to be grasping badminton rackets. I eyed some comfy hammocks tucked away in the shade beside what I recognized from a hot-springs retreat brochure as a sweat lodge.

It should be noted at this juncture that there is very little woo-woo in me. There's plenty of yahoo, more than enough pooh-pooh, and at any given time that refreshing drink food, Yoo-Hoo, washing through my system, but barely a trace of woo-woo. When a New Ager begins to describe the healing power of crystals, I say, "Yes, but how many cleaning flushes will these provide the bowl before they'll need to be replaced?"

It's not all their half-baked psychobabble, their earnestness, their lack of regular bathing (that would be the pot calling the kettle black, in my case), those Zoloft-laced smiles, or even their tendency to stock their music collections with Peruvian pan flute music and every recording Enya has ever made. It's that complete loss of humor many New Agers inherit when they start down their path.

Fortunately, I would discover that it's hard not to laugh easily at life when you're in your birthday suit holding a spatula mere feet from an open flame. So I left my woo-woo bias at the picnic table with my bike helmet while not focusing too hard on these nude, and in several instances nubile, bodies in all their hairy glory.

I beat a path for the Jacuzzi. It had been a tiring ride, not to mention that the tub would provide a bit of modesty while I adjusted to the fact that I was actually in a nudist colony. I was, for all practical purposes, a nudist myself. No matter how open-minded you may think you are as you roll through your days, standing without a shred of clothing at a garden party of nude people can't help but bring up the dreaded naked-on-test-day nightmare. You know the one— everyone's had it. But no one seemed to be giving the nakedness thing much energy, so that helped. A man named Rainsong, basking in the sunshine next to the tub, asked his life partner, Harmony, to track down their boy, Cauliflower. Cauliflower? I kid you not. In my estimation, such a name forecasted a protracted and especially angst-ridden adolescence. That, or the young man would learn to mold his fists into weapons of mass destruction before the second grade. Breaking the name up might help a little. Cauli could be Cal, for short. Or he might want to work with Flower—more problematic, but it too could be chopped down to Flo, sort of hip and sports-related. Cauliflower came running over. He struck me as a perfectly content child of ten. His handshake was firm, his demeanor polite and confident. Cauliflower dashed off to dig for worms with other kids—what I quickly named the "produce section" of the colony.

Looking around from my spot in the tub, another point of interest caught my eye. There's something slightly disconcerting about dreadlocks on white men. Remember how unnatural it was when those chimps were dressed up in toddler clothes during Disney movies? That's how I feel every time I see a white guy from the suburbs sporting tentacles of foot-long, uncombed hair. On a black man it's regal and right; on Steve or Stewart it's as foolish as clown's paint.

Dreadlock Man came over. The cool beverage he carried was for me. He turned out to be as pleasant a gent as you could ask for. I concluded that if you're going to spend time with a bunch of naked people, it helps if they all have those great Australian accents. There's something proper and at the same time relaxing about their speech patterns. Damn it if these people weren't making it difficult for me to poke fun at them. I met Dreadlock Man's smile.

"Let me ask you something." I gestured to the Eden-like scene sprawled across the grounds of his colony. "It's a work week and not a holiday in sight unless there's some sort of Boxing Day celebration I wasn't aware of, so are these folks independently wealthy with tutors for their kids? You can't tell me all of them are on vacation."

Dreadlock Man nodded. "You've arrived just in time for the wedding. Four days of fun with the ceremony on Saturday at sunset."

As he pointed out the bride and groom (I'd be able to

identify the guy in a blinding snowstorm by his ample back hair and the woman by the tasteful tattoo of a boomerang etched just below the small of her back), I mourned the fact that we were only staying for lunch.

"Nonsense, mate. Digger has you slated to share some of your stories tonight at the fire circle. He called you quite the raconteur."

Some people might be resistant to the stroking of their ego, but for me it does the trick every time. Maybe I'd perform the one where I'm treed by geese in New Hampshire.

"Have you seen the buffet?" Shane exclaimed.

"We're staying for the wedding," I announced. "Digger's the best man, and the dude with all the dreadlocks—"

"Roger," Norbu interjected.

"Roger made us a formal invite."

"Then I'm going to need to borrow some sunscreen," Shane said.

I still couldn't look directly at the panoramic version of Shane, but I could see out of the corner of my eye that he was getting a little pink in places. That, and he'd abandoned his tea somewhere along the way. Come to think of it, I could use a wide-brimmed hat.

"Don't ask me to help you apply it," I joked.

"I think I still remember how to reach those spots," he countered.

It was going to be a choice weekend. I wandered over to see how the tofu burgers were coming along.

■■■■

While I can't say I would sign up as a lifetime member of the International Naturalism Federation, my time in the

colony was not the decadent Roman holiday I'd always suspected it would be. There's plenty of truth to the idea that a
body part partially covered is quite tantalizing but a completely naked man or woman collecting dirty dishes from a
picnic table or testing the pool for the proper amount of
chlorine is routine, mundane even.

The wedding was beautiful—simple, with the emphasis
on the bride and groom's feelings about each other. The radiant weather, paths of flower petals marking their way,
and Mambo Kings music made the reception bounce and
swing. I was one of the few in attendance fully dressed.
This was due not to a sudden bout of modesty but to forgetting to heed the good advice of the Alabama Slamma. It's
shocking how a sunburn can sneak up like that. I did manage to dance, even with several soothing sticks of aloe vera
plants shoved down my pants. You have to make conces-
sions when a live band's trumpet and percussion sections
work everyone into a stupor with a rowdy rendition of
"Pueblo Nuevo."

"It's really going to smart when you have to get back on
your bike." Norbu was having some fun at my expense.

I had another drink, deposited some of the ice down my
shorts for good measure, and watched the happy couple cut
their cake. Does it really matter whether you take those
vows in your birthday suit or buttoned up tight in matching
snow pants and parkas? At the time, I was years away from
meeting my own true love, so I had no words of wisdom for
the beaming bride and gallant groom. I'm sure I could have
made something up that sounded sweet and optimistic, but
really, who would take seriously the words of a twenty-
something Yank with aloe vera sticking out of his britches?

I remember toasting them at one point in my mind, something about health, wealth, and a lifetime of successful electrolysis.

Nearly a decade into my own marriage now, I have learned a few things, but if I could return to the feet of that unclothed couple, I still wouldn't presume to read the landscape of anyone else's relationship but my own. I tell you, some days it's like being Helen Keller at a jigsaw puzzle convention. If anything, maybe I picked up a few tips that naked weekend that have come in handy. Don't dress yourselves in too many plans for the future, because it has a way of robbing strength from the moment. And if you're hell bent on hiding your feelings in private places, you might as well just live alone. Oh, and remember to dust off Mambo Kings music at every party, anniversary, and reunion. More marriages have been saved by a good horn section than you would think.

━━━■━━■━━

"Makes me wonder if anyone's ever done an extended bike tour naked." Norbu had enjoyed his weekend in the sun a little too much.

"I'm not riding behind you unless you're wearing pants," said Alabama Shane.

"I'm not riding behind either of you. It's too painful after what I saw this week," Norbu replied.

We hit the road, fully clothed, but each of us sporting an entirely new sense of freedom.

WE'LL FIND YOUR BALLS
COME SPRINGTIME

If you're gonna leave your balls out in the snow, Alaska is as keen a place as any—better than most, actually. But for why and how I happened to find myself in such a state, we should backpedal a bit, to the top of Kicking Horse Pass, a beatific, lonesome stretch of permafrost road located a tad to the south and east, in the slightly tamer wilds of Canada. I'm taking you back to when life was simply a matter of finding a comfy cadence and pacing myself and the bicycle through the crisp April air of a British Columbia morning.

This was before the forest fire or the lawyer from New Zealand who wouldn't stop bragging about his IQ. The Brazilian runway model who felt she'd just die if she didn't get her helicopter ride to see those cute blue glaciers. And long before the hypothermic Brit who insisted, in proper queen's English, that I capture him on film attempting to freeze to death in a flimsy windbreaker on top of a sizable mountain.

Kicking Horse Pass would be the spot on the map where I lost what little was left of my impulse control. Where I decided to extend a short Canadian bike ride into a full-blown odyssey across the Big Outside. Alaska in April, baby.

A mini-epiphany struck me on that hilltop. I saw with early-morning clarity that every long curve I've ever navigated, every tight sloping angle when I've hung rubber just this side of the yellow line, only inches from oncoming traffic or the edge of the abyss, has a story behind it.

No one simply materializes at the top of the hill.

But only if you keep going. It takes effort, a certain elemental commitment to get yourself and that rolling metal steed up the mountain. It involves sweat, concentration, and no small measure of faith. There's also the fervent belief that there will be this sweet-as-honey downhill run waiting just after the crest, the promise of an amazing, if brief, boundless glide to the bottom.

And between the peaks and valleys are the people: gloriously screwed-up people waiting for me to get to know them. Such knowledge filled me with tent-revival-level inspiration and an almost blind determination. I kept heading north despite good sense and a rudimentary grasp of meteorology.

Maybe the fact that I was far from ready to rejoin the working week played some part in my decision. Dictators the world over understand the underlying problem with freedom; it's as addictive as the purest Afghan-grown poppy. And bike-touring freedom . . . well now, that's in an endorphin-fueled class by itself. No twelve-step program on earth exists to break its hold once the road finds your name.

In short, I can reach for any excuse to extend a bike tour. And the phrase "the other side of the mountain" had a melodic, if not slightly Romper Room, ring to it. Besides, Alaska had been on my to-do list for years. I couldn't let a little thing like the wrong time of year stop me.

While climbing Kicking Horse Pass I met up with a forest ranger, a Paul Bunyan type in Gore-Tex and gloves out for a day ride. He was hammering the highway to his job near Jasper. His face did not register alarm when I told him my freshly concocted plans to be the first guy at the gates of Denali National Park that year, but he did inquire if I had some sort of transponder device on board in case they had to locate my body through deep snow, ice, or both.

The things that count as humor in the Park Service.

As we worked a good rhythm together in pursuit of the top, the spin of our freewheels didn't startle a collection of high-country goats in the least. One or two gave us casual glances, but they moved less than a millimeter from the task of munching on spring grass that was sprouting between the permafrost cracks right down the center of the Trans-Canada Highway, which runs through Banff National Park. It was one of the first natural indications of the season, though banks of snow were piled two stories high in places, deep and solid along the sides of this recently opened road. While straddling my bike and fighting back the burn of cold air stabbing overworked lungs, I dug out my camera and snapped photos of these hulking goats, just so friends didn't think I was telling wild-animal tales again. And the goats? If given opposable thumbs and modern technology, they might have clicked off a couple shots of us to show the rest of the herd back home just how irresponsibly independent some humans on two wheels can act when left to their own devices.

The ranger, goats, and I weren't alone on this popular (in the summertime) stretch of highway. Earlier, I'd witnessed a busload of Japanese tourists sporting woefully inappropriate footwear, cameras at the ready, stumble and slide along the frozen banks of Lake Louise, while behind them the peaks of Mounts Hector, Columbia, and Lyell stood like frosted cathedrals in the afternoon sun. It was as if Charlie Chaplin had staged a scene inside an Ansel Adams photograph. Watching the whole affair from across the lake brought me great joy.

I added another layer of polypropylene. I'm the sort of guy who gets all bothered if the hot water runs out in the shower. I guess I *really* didn't want to head south for home, work, routine . . . boredom. We stepped up the cadence. My plan was to make it miles beyond Kicking Horse Pass by nightfall. I had only the vaguest idea where I was going, but miles from the top of an unprotected pass would be nice. With reliable forecasts coming out of the northern latitudes that predicted spring had not truly sprung yet, I took in a deep, arrogant breath of disregard, chased it down with high-tech winter fabrics and an inflated sense of my abilities, then tucked myself into a tight ball for the bracing whiplash descent.

The Alaska Marine Highway was only a few hundred miles to the west. I could board a ferry, ride the waterway like a hobo hopping the rails all the way to Skagway or Haines, pedal through bald eagle country along the coast, then work up the desolate Yukon Highway until it connected with the Alaska Highway. From there it was a slushy, gravel-bitten, on-road, off-road, no-road push-and-drag all the way to the heart of the state. Unless a grizzly waking up for the season ate me first. Folks are forever telling me it's good thinking to have a backup plan, and that one seemed to adhere nicely to an environmentally correct cycle of life.

"Just so you know, grizzlies rarely eat people. Usually they'll just bat you around until your limbs fly off or you bleed out," said the ranger.

This tour extension to Alaska was inspired madness. There's a giddiness that flows unabated right after the cementing of a risky decision on a bike tour. The euphoria comes on because your choice hasn't cost you anything of value yet. Nonetheless, the ranger's info about griz behavior was a disturbing piece of trivia.

"And most people start in Denali around June and ride south," he added.

"Most people . . ." I was trying to think of something clever to say, but by the time I came up with it the wind chill made me choke back my words. Silent and focused, we barreled over the hill into the ice blues and cobalt blacks of dusk.

I stood at the dock, stomping my legs to check that my blood hadn't frozen to gum in the predawn light. I was pondering things over. The Alaska Marine Highway is a vast waterway, and unless I was able to carve myself a set of pontoons from the towering old-growth forest behind me before departure time, I would have to board the boat. Alaska being an add-on to my tour, I'd abruptly shifted into war rations mode when it came to parting with my rapidly shrinking collection of dead presidents. To that point, I'd played hard and fast, spending my way across Canada like a political candidate awash in soft money, spreading good cheer and generosity in campground, hostel, and bar alike in an attempt to be the neighbor to the south who would be welcomed back soon and often—the life of the party. Now I had to get creative or get on a bus for home.

If I paid for a ticket outright, it could be a fatal fiscal blow. This being primarily a car ferry, though, if I managed to piggyback onto someone's car/passenger package, I could float for a fraction of the price. I needed to make some friends or I'd be down to one meal a day traveling in a hurry.

Here's the thing I never understood about that fable of the grasshopper and the ant. The grasshopper, he lives it up all summer, plays his fiddle for the busy ants from time to time; come winter, though, the ants grumble a little and take him to task but let him in before the hopper feels much pain.

What's the lesson? Ants are the Mother Teresas of the insect world? It pays to know how to play a party instrument like the fiddle over, say, the tuba or, God forbid, the triangle? If you're lazy, you'd damn well better be charming? I remember this librarian at a kids' story hour saying that the grasshopper learned not to leave anything to chance or the last minute for fear of freezing to death.

That's not how I saw it.

The other kids nodded, properly frightened, if not by the hopper's recklessness, then by the notion of becoming an ice cube when so many good fiddling years were ahead of them. The group became ants before my eyes.

My eight-year-old hand went into the air. I wish I'd been

equipped to express that the hopper represented freedom and the ants conformity. That a balance always needs to be struck between totalitarianism and anarchy without the loss of personal exploration because therein lies our only hope for flashes of genius and emotional evolution. We must let homeless malcontents wander among the suits and ties because it is the essence of democracy and the cornerstone of any free, thriving society.

"I liked the grasshopper." This was all I managed to articulate before the rush for cookies and juice ended further discussion.

A pale girl who never went anywhere without a science book under her sweaty armpit stood behind me in the snack line. "Correct me if I'm wrong, but don't grasshoppers eat ants?!"

At least someone else was thinking outside the box.

Years later I realized that our little story hour had damaged me to my core. I happily embarked down a brash, unrepentant path, lonely and cold at times but filled with optimism, faith in my figurative fiddle playing, and a belief that everyone, deep down, wants to be reminded how to have a good time.

But the grasshopper way of life was meeting fierce resistance on the docks above Prince Rupert Sound. Most of the cars were packed to the gills with furniture and luggage. These travelers, even if they wanted to do me a solid, couldn't make room for another passenger, especially one with a loaded bicycle. Battered but not defeated, I decided to rest my feet next to a raging game of Hacky Sack. These guys certainly knew how to stay warm.

"You want in?" one of the players eventually asked.

"If you don't mind risking the sack going into the water."

I wasn't that bad, but I wanted to cover myself just in case. Hacky Sacks tend to be very personal items to certain players, and it can be traumatic if a stranger destroys the one you've been playing with for years. I learned this firsthand around a late-night campfire in Chimayo, New Mexico.

These guys were so good that my game didn't affect the flow much. I was having a good deal of fun, so much that as the sun came up over the water I'd nearly forgotten that I would be parting with the bulk of my cash in mere minutes.

My Hacky partners worked for a moving company. I told them they should forget the job and go pro on the Hacky circuit. "You should see the game Ben usually brings to our circle," one replied. "He's like a Harlem Globetrotter of the Hacky world."

We worked a tricky volley in silence. Once the sack was back on a rhythm, the player to my left—his shirt told me his name was Jim—said, "We had to leave Ben back in Medicine Hat. He swelled up like a blowfish from some bad clams or something." Turning to the hacker to his left: "You did call last night to make sure he's still on the mend, right?"

I let the sack drop. Ben was going to be fine. "Tell me something, guys. Did your company already buy Ben a ticket on this ferry?"

My bike was stowed with the rest of the family posses-

sions for a forestry professor from Juneau, and I rode onto
the ship in the front cab of a moving van. Ben's shirt fit a little snugly, but this grasshopper felt free and unburdened
once more.

I offered to buy the boys their first round.

The ferry ride, all three days of it, was well worth the
price of the ticket I hadn't paid for. Whales surfaced off the
starboard bow, making their way back from winter vacation along Mexico's Baja peninsula. Their tails smacked the
choppy water, weighty and wide, reminding me of a castle
door slamming closed against an invading army. See, if the
whales didn't think it was too early in the season to head
north, what was I fretting about? The captain informed the
passengers of their good fortune: "It's the first stretch of two
consecutive clear days this year." I pretended not to hear
that and focused on one of my top ten sunsets of all time.
Light skated along the horizon while a pack of porpoises
chased the ship's wake and caribou stood as silent sentinels
along the wooded, rocky shores. We slept on Astroturf under
huge stand-up heaters positioned along the covered portion
of the top deck. Many of the passengers tried to get comfortable in plastic lawn chairs, but I chose to lay my sleeping bag on the par-four turf and study the stars up in their
icy heaven.

In Haines, I pedaled right off the ship and down the
gangplank buoyed by the weather and my good luck so far.
I waved good-bye to my Hacky Sack heroes and some new
fish-cannery friends driving an ancient convertible Cadillac
with suicide doors—the same model that John F. Kennedy
rode into history on that Dallas morning.

The narrow lane of pavement cut right through a bald eagle preserve, among mammoth trees crowding a fast-running river. There were so many eagle's nests constructed high in leafless trees that I turned finding them into something of a game. The occasional rolling hill offered a bit of gear work, but for the most part I cruised effortlessly and unmolested by traffic or fellow tourists. So this was what it felt like to be king for a day. I surveyed my lands and wanted for nothing. That evening I stayed in a converted officer's quarters/bed-and-breakfast that overlooked the water. Two uni-browed ladies—sisters, I believed—seemed surprised to see me, or anyone, roll up to their wraparound porch. But maybe that was just how they always appeared. At first the sisters insisted they weren't open for the season, but I stayed put until one of them convinced the other that the bed would just lie empty otherwise. Alaskans don't always choose commerce over privacy. I was told not to expect hot water in the shower. That was the last I saw of the pair. Breakfast came in the form of a bag of tea I rummaged up from the table by the front door. I slipped out into another brisk, cloudless morning. My only desire now was a little companionship.

Along came Rusty.

The way I was carrying on, you'd swear we'd been lost in the wilderness for days. Though I had maps, panniers full of supplies, and only the one strip of blacktop to follow, doubt crept in during treacherously rough days navigating bikes over the snow-swept reaches of the Yukon Highway, then the pothole-littered depths of the Alaska Highway. At one point I was wearing every article of clothing I owned. The term *highway* should be considered in only the broadest sense. If we pedaled for more than a mile of continuously paved roadtop I'd howl with joy. The next series of potholes or a completely washed-out section stifled those celebrations in a hurry. When I relate that it was a horrid road, with unpredictable weather and biting winds for the better part of a week, this is not tongue-in-cheek, bike-touring travelogue bravado. It was absolutely brutal work of the sweatshop variety, maybe twenty-five miles of progress a day. I fell asleep in my riding clothes right after dinner three nights in a row.

Rusty was the perfect traveling companion for this unexpected test of endurance and sanity. Due to a past peppered with abundant hits of acid or the possibility that he'd actually discovered the meaning of life upon the seven hundredth playing of Pink Floyd's "Dark Side of the Moon," nothing bothered Rusty. He was out for a ride, plain and simple. If old even-steven Rusty, in his oversized pilot's jacket, were to pedal through the gates of hell, I'd expect he'd remain at room temperature, maybe bum a smoke off the devil, ask for directions, and be on his way. Unable to attain anything resembling this level of cool, I still had to admire it.

"What sort of bear you make that for?" Rusty asked.

We'd been resting over our handlebars somewhere between Burwash Landing and Beaver Creek. I was using my down time to count how many seconds it took the beads of sweat rolling down the bridge of my nose to crystallize into ice. With the wind chill factor, it had to be no more than 10 degrees Fahrenheit. The ice crystal record so far stood at three seconds.

"It's either a brown bear on steroids or one of those

chummy things they call . . . um . . . a grizzly." Excellent—I was going to get to put the ranger's trivia regarding bear attacks to an actual field test. My body was too damn tired to react properly. Instead of breaking into a two-wheeled sprint, I remained static, letting frost build on my cheeks and chin.

The beast rocked back and forth on all fours as if he were listening to music at a higher frequency. It struck me as something I'd seen before, not on the Learning Channel but the dance floor at a college club packed with frat boys on nickel beer nights.

Jesus. Next to me Rusty had begun to rock in the same fashion, left and right in a series of motions over his handlebars. Someone needed to inform the space cowboy that we were not at a Grateful Dead concert. They danced like that for two or three minutes, a Fox special that I hoped wasn't titled *When Animals with Bluesy Rhythm Attack*. Discounting the presence of a several-thousand-pound animal that was either preparing to charge us or perhaps mate with Rusty, the patches of snow latticed between incandescent moss and sunlight angling through the big trees was actually quite striking and almost otherworldly. Coming back to matters at hand, I comforted myself with the fact that at least we were wearing helmets. Maybe the funerals would be open-casket.

The griz finally slowed down this hip-hop party. He then backed almost silently into the bush. I was dumbfounded. Rusty turned to me.

"That was so stellar."

"No, that was completely insane," I corrected.

"Same difference."

Sometimes you have to take chances. Rusty, of course, was the equivalent of a pair of tumbling dice, so I wasn't about to look to him for my missing impulse control. But when we met Mark along a fork of the Alaska Highway and the road to Valdez, again I threw plans to the wind. His truck was stacked with sea kayaks. I fell into step, loading my bike beside Rusty's and taking a thin sliver on the bench seat in the cab. The tourist season hadn't started yet, and Mark was going out to do some scouting. We were welcome to come along, free of charge.

It felt good to be heading south for a while. Denali would still be there in the morning, and how long until a chance to paddle the killing grounds of one of the country's largest oil spills presented itself again? Not to mention that the truck's cab was nice and toasty. We motored for Prince William Sound.

Unlike disasters that take the lives of large numbers of humans, few honor and fewer still even remember the sea birds and water creatures that were choked out of existence by an oil company choosing profit over double-hulled protection. Mark was a walking textbook about the spill. He'd plucked dozens of birds from the water before the company response teams were even able to pronounce "plausible deniability." Today, oil still exists in large quantities just under the rocks and in the soil along the coast.

"Maybe they learned something," Mark said as we paddled the inlets and hugged island coves. "But my guess is the lesson only went as far as which company carries the best insurance riders, and no farther."

It was easy to see why someone could hold a grudge. A drop-dead-gorgeous spot on the planet had been saturated in oil. Cleaned on the surface, but who knew the long-term effects on things unseen?

"I scrubbed rocks and stones along these beaches until my fingers bled," Mark said.

It looked pristine now, but then I had no point of reference from before the spill.

"It's like a bone after a bad break. You always feel it. Even if no one else can tell."

"Who wants to play a round of golf?" Mark made this query while driving us to his parents' house north of Anchorage. Funny, he'd struck me as more of a Green Party member than a greens fee sort of fellow. Cool and collected Rusty appeared shaken for the first time in our travels together, as though he'd just been asked to murder family members in their sleep. Where had our eco-friendly kayaker gone? Besides, the three of us, looking as we did, wouldn't have lasted fifteen seconds on the grounds of a country club before someone placed a quiet cell phone call to their private police force.

"Uh, I'm mostly a putt-putt guy," I said, which was true. I can put it in the turtle's mouth, one stroke every time.

"Wait, before you shoot it down . . . I think you'll like this course." Mark tried to contain a smile as we pulled into the driveway of his folks' spread, an understated cabin-style home on the edge of a frozen lake. It was the house of my lumberjack dreams. A solar-powered hot tub was the first thing I noticed as we took the deck two steps at a time. Okay, maybe a lumberjack with a subscription to *Martha Stewart Living,* but it was a killer setup nonetheless. The sharp aroma of a wood fire reached my nose before the heavy door closed. Burly mushing dogs greeted us a few feet ahead of Mark's parents.

"This is Cain and Abel." I didn't know if Mark was talking about the dogs or his parents. He'd explained on the drive up that he had been raised by two dads. "And to answer the question I get far too often: No, having gay parents did not turn me into a homosexual." He'd shaken his head while a sardonic look took up residence on his face. "Like people think it's a club or something that's always pounding doors for new members." Obviously Mark had some issues surrounding the whole thing—maybe not his folks' sexual preferences, but certainly some of his Alaskan neighbors' more Neanderthal opinions on the subject.

"Hey, I was raised by a numerologist and a woman who swore she was Stevie Nicks," Rusty had noted. "It didn't make me see messages in bar codes or want to wear long skirts and lace gloves everywhere."

"Thank God for that," I'd said. "You wandering around dressed as a Gypsy woman, searching for answers on bus schedules and lottery tickets—now that's a damn frightful image."

Bruce and Roy were wonderful hosts. Around eight that evening we finished off the largest slab of barbecued ribs I've ever had the good fortune to be in the presence of. Afterward we took up golf clubs and wandered down to the frozen lake. It was ten o'clock at night, but bright as midday.

Holes half a foot deep had been cut into the ice, and Day-Glo golf balls you could spot clear across the lake lay waiting for us to whack. Homemade flags marked the various "greens." My first steps onto the ice were tentative, but soon I could be observed sliding across nature's tabletop finish like Fred Astaire.

I will say that a brisk round of ice golf while the sun hangs steady above the horizon a couple of hours before midnight is as much fun as sex outdoors in the summertime. Any dark and whispery doubts and demons you carry onto the ice dissipate when you land that first clean smack on the face of the ball. As we approached the flag for the fourth hole, I asked if that was a drink cooler near the "green." That it was, and it had companions, situated at strategic places along the course. The cooler kept the beer inside from freezing—most of the time.

My game, never a threat to anyone on the PGA circuit, deteriorated precipitously after a third barley-tainted beverage. When I managed to whack my fourth or fifth golf ball, a bright yellow number, into the deep snow outside the natural boundary of the lake, Bruce assured me that it was not a problem.

"We'll find your balls come springtime," he announced.

"I thought this *was* springtime."

Even Rusty was laughing at me now.

"Springtime starts around the first week in June," Roy explained. "And winter can settle back in as early as the last week in September."

I had to ask. "And what about summer?"

"It makes an appearance for a few hours in August," Mark said. "At least that's what we've agreed to tell the tourists who show up while the lakes are still frozen over."

On the eighteenth hole Bruce and Roy regaled us with stories about the Pillar Mountain Golf Classic they'd attended recently in Kodiak on April Fool's Day. The course, a one-hole par seventy, is actually a 1,400-foot mountain you slash and chop your way up. The weather can turn so nasty that players are told to bring crampons, usually reserved for mountaineering. And if you forget your gloves, you could be looking at digit-removing frostbite.

"It's guerrilla golf at its finest. I shot about a six hundred," Bruce confessed. "And lost more balls than I could count." He nodded. "So you see, Joe, someone will probably find my balls come springtime as well."

The next afternoon we hauled out the bicycles and pedaled right onto the frozen lake. Who could tell what time it really was? Bruce turned up the stereo. Using clubs, drivers, putters, and snow shovels, we invented a bastardized version of polo, our bikes substituting for horses. Sliding, skidding, pedaling furiously for purchase, and occasionally smacking into the slushy banks, we played with the abandon of kids on the corner before their mothers call them home for dinner or the flicker of the streetlight chases them from the curbs. Deep into the sun-drenched night we yelped and spun until a silent snowfall and waning light finally halted the game. I stood over my bicycle, head back to the heavens, glad to be staying in one place for more than a day.

While my body cooled down I also thanked whoever it was who had given me this stingy supply of impulse control. I was still determined to make it to the gates of

Denali National Park, first foolish tourist of the season—a salmon swimming against the cold, cold current. But in the meantime, I could sure use some hot chocolate, a roaring fire, and maybe a big sledding dog to sleep beside. Hey, there's a fine line between self-control and freezing to death. And I still knew the difference.

FAST FOOD
IN THE WORLD'S SLOW LANES

Cyclists don't dine, they feed.
—ANONYMOUS RIDER

Fast food is like trying to date cheap ladies in bad lighting.

They look good enough to eat, hot and easy to approach under the right conditions, but outside their natural environment they cool down quickly and can turn ugly, and while you might walk away feeling queasy and possibly diseased, you rarely leave with satisfaction.

Still, people keep coming back for more. Like so many things, we've bought the myth of speed over substance. And if they'll supersize that baby, put it on a 99-cent menu, and cook it in the right amount of lard, we'll choke down anything this side of battery acid or barnacle waste and call it good.

But I'm not here to curse an industry that boasts billions and billions served and fronts clowns and barn animals as spokespeople. That's child's play. There's also the nagging fact that I've consumed too many double combos and hot apple "pies" during my bike travels to go righteous on the subject.

No, what's important here is the mishaps and mischief I've pedaled into while a guest at these establishments. That, and the way big-name burger huts and chicken stands have failed so grandly in certain parts of the world when it comes to rushing other cultures through their meals.

In Ireland, until they add stools and dart boards and tap some Guinness, fast food doesn't stand a chance in hell of supplanting the local pub. The concept of fast anything just goes against every fiber of an Irishman's leisurely and gregarious soul.

The same goes for many of the islands. On Aruba, a spit of sand and leisure that at most is sixty miles long and ten miles wide, if you asked for a to-go order, they'd laugh and reply, "To go where?" Ten years' worth of Styrofoam cartons, unused, lay stacked up behind the local McDonald's. And the last time I cruised Bon Bini on my bike, it was hard to order anything very fast or even at all during the afternoon siesta. In Venezuela, I actually climbed behind the counter of a dilapidated roadside ice cream kiosk, figured out how to work the ancient but cold soft-serve machine, and left some change on top of a crate. At least, I think it was soft serve.

Let's call it fast food adventures in the world's slow lanes. The disturbing fact is that there are more and more burger boxes and Taco Bells sprouting up along even some of the thinner roads on the map, and much as I try, I can't be helping the situation. When my blood sugar drops, pitifully and always regrettably I become part of the problem, influenced as it were by my own weaknesses, those bright colors, and the petite prices.

In my defense, though, I've gone weeks without as much as a fry touching my lips. A peek inside my panniers on any given day of healthy chowing might reveal the following food products:

RICE

GORP (good old raisins and peanuts)

BEANS

FIRM FRUITS (apples and oranges)

FIRM VEGGIES (peppers, mushrooms, etc.)

TORTILLAS (regular bread gets crushed like
 Bill Gates back on the elementary-school
 playground)

CHEESE BLOCKS (defying conventional wisdom,
 cheese does not need to stay cool)

PACKAGED CHEESE STICKS (not so healthy but easier
 to eat on the fly than those whole blocks)

POTATOES (or "potatos" if you're drafting with
 former VP Dan Quayle)

JERKY

PEANUT BUTTER (crunchy, because smooth turns
 into a river on warm days)

And my dearest friend, PASTA

It's long past time that I make a public plea for pasta as the official king of all road food. I've been known to cook up a pot of pasta—angel hair or elbows, ziti or shells—with the leftover boiling water from my morning tea. What I'll do is drop it into a Ziploc bag, toss in a stick or more of butter (that's right—cyclists aren't afraid of a little cholesterol), some seasoning, then shake until the noodles are practically swimming. Then I'll wrap it inside some foil to keep it warm and place it in my front bag. When the inevitable fade arrives midmorning, I just stop, lean over my handlebars, and open up what I lovingly call my "pasta pouch" (patent pending). I don't even get off the bike. It's amazing how often it's still piping hot. If I'm feeling ambitious, I'll wrap the Ziploc bag and foil inside a winter glove to give it more insulation.

What I appreciate are the looks I receive from drivers who spot me hanging over the front bag, a fork blazing as I shovel noodles.

"Marge, I'm not sure but I believe that young man was hoisting mounds of fettuccine Alfredo out of his camera bag. Maybe you should drive for a while."

One morning, after a brutally long climb, I actually attempted to fork some pasta while coasting along at a decent clip. This proved a mistake. Fortunately, the silverware did not punch its way completely through my cheek, but it did a number on the inside of my mouth. Had it been a larger pothole I'd bounced through, I'm certain I could have found work in a punk band or maybe in a sideshow as Fork Boy— step right up and see actual utensils growing out of his flesh.

Sometimes the need for food clouds my judgment. And just where the hell was I going on a bike tour that I couldn't stop for a minute or two and gorge myself on pasta by the side of the road like any other red-blooded, sane touring cyclist?

But it was a man named Sebastian who taught me the true value of empty calories and just how much a cyclist can get away with consuming if he pedals long and hard and carries enough weight in his panniers.

We'd hooked up as ride partners down on New Zealand's South Island. He didn't act like an engineer. For one thing, he was damn funny. And Sebastian was also imbued with a healthy amount of emotional flexibility—another trait not often found in engineers. He credited the complete annihilation of his heart, courtesy of his first wife, for this buoyancy of character.

"After that whole miserable experience, it clicked one day that in some cases the world doesn't want to add up no matter how hard one tries." Sebastian cracked his knuckles. "It took some of the pressure off, you know?"

We looked over miles of shockingly green South Island's pastureland. I nodded.

"She told me I lacked passion."

Again the knuckles went off like snap peas: one, two, three.

"Maybe she was on to something. But people . . . I believe they can change, you know?"

He was the one riding the loaded bike across a distant island nation, so the argument carried water with me.

Now, the way his bike was loaded *did* strike me as the work of an engineer. It was buttoned up airtight. No stray parts or pieces dangling, no half-empty water jugs or miscellaneous debris of any sort strapped on with threadbare bungee cords. If you were to place his load and mine side by side, it would have represented the Odd Couple of the cycling community.

"You mind a little company?" he asked.

I took one more look at his shipshape packing job, then settled my eyes back on his face. I wanted to believe it belonged to a man who had given up judging others long ago.

"Not at all. I just said good-bye to my barber. He's gonna keep pedaling along the coast."

"Your barber goes on tour with you?" Sebastian appeared fairly confused by this one. I don't think I struck him at first glance as an aristocrat. Nor at second or third glance.

"No, no. Well, in this case, yes. I met Roberto last week outside of Wellington. Roberto's a whole other story, but it's safe to say that over the long haul I tour solo, no posse, no entourage, and definitely no sag wagon."

"That's the only way to go," agreed Sebastian. The knuckle snapping was becoming more of a punctuation device when he spoke. "But if means anything, your hair really looks good."

As bikers, the joke had more punch. We shared a solid laugh, decided in short order to take to the road for a while, and pedaled our newly formed two-man pace line for the high country.

"We could chop up some onions to give tonight's stew a little kick," I offered. Stew had been our featured entree for the third evening in a row.

"You have an onion?" Sebastian asked, a bit of culinary hope momentarily flushing his cheeks.

"Uh . . . no. I was just thinking how nice that would taste. Wait, there might be a few packets of onion salt at the bottom of my pannier."

In New Zealand, if you stick to the perimeter roads, the main arteries that circle the North and South Islands, you'll run into a pub, café, or store every twenty miles or so. But head into the wilds of this unfettered land and you are utterly on your own. To any real adventure seeker on two wheels, Ritz means a cracker, not a hotel. Depending on your pace and the unpredictable whims of the weather gods, it can be several days before you come upon shelter, a good meal, or any food that isn't still using its legs to run away from you.

"Show me again how many Wendy's combo meals I could burn off per day at my current pace."

We weren't in a campground per se because the majority of New Zealand is more or less one big nature preserve. Hanging up formal campground signs would be somewhat redundant.

It was now evening four without a store to replenish our kitchens, so we'd been reduced to eating weird combinations of foods from our combined stock. These menus, which I took to describing like a pretentious waiter at an overpriced bistro, included macaroni and cheese garnished with sun-dried raisins and shelled walnuts. Lightly braised Wheat Thin smothered in peanut butter and topped with the island's premium processed tomato product (which we'd swiped from the condiments jar at an Auckland eatery). Slow-aged (inside my panniers) beef jerky dipped in sweet grape jelly (from petite packets also swiped from a café somewhere on the North Island).

I pulled out an old copy of Edward Abbey's *Desert Solitaire.* It had once been dropped into a pot of lentil soup, rescued, then covered with milkshakes, coffee, and so many other food products that my plan of last resort has always been to cook the flavor-soaked pages at a slow rolling boil with some minced celery and garlic if I happen to have any on hand. It hadn't come down to eating one of my favorite authors yet, but our food stocks were getting frighteningly low.

One thing you'll never find in my bags is a banana. If

I've learned nothing else from all my miles in the saddle it's this: bananas should be consumed on the spot. If you must take them to go, allow the Chiquita or the Dole to ride in the front handlebar bag only, and monitor its whereabouts at all times and with a vigilance bordering on paranoia. I've seen too many banana-gone-bad incidents in my day. We were frantically searching for something else to throw onto the menu when Sebastian called me over to examine what he thought was the aftermath of raccoons defecating into his left rear pannier. It was certainly a rancid mess, one truly putrid sight. Like studying NEA-funded art in a hip SoHo gallery, we were thoroughly puzzled until, with the tip of a fork, I located that familiar little sticker, which hadn't yet completely decomposed. It turned out to be a bunch of Dole's finest he'd purchased in Hawaii on a layover a few weeks before. "In the Congo, they'd boil up those peels and make a nice beer out of the whole thing," I offered. "Or they'd just smoke 'em."

"And in the Andes plane crash survivors had to eat the frozen carcasses of their friends," Sebastian replied, gingerly tossing the bananas over the ridge. "But my hunger has a long way to go before we salvage those bananas or start gnawing away at each other's ankles."

My stomach growled.

"Have you ever read any Edward Abbey?" I brought out my copy of *Desert Solitaire* and gave him a whiff. My pal conceded that it smelled better than dinner.

"If we don't find a store tomorrow, it's what's on the menu."

As we ate, Sebastian fired up his laptop computer so we could see what we were missing. He began running this outrageous calorie-counting program, proving his engineering credentials with a certain flair that again I found delightfully unbecoming the average man of science and technology. He confessed that a colleague had loaded it onto the machine in a protective move, in case Seb was ever in need of a calorie counter while trapped on a desert island.

"In any other country, the information I'm about to reveal could turn us into bloated fast-food troglodytes, but I think . . ." He held up a Ritz cracker and my copy of *Desert Solitaire* to make his point. "We're pretty safe from temptation way out here. Let's have a look, shall we?"

Sebastian was like a kid with the newest toy on the block. He printed a list that he read out loud, crazed-MIT-grad-student style, hand gestures and all. The woodland creatures and I took note as the computer quietly spit out page after page of data.

"How much extra paper do you carry on board?" Sebastian ignored this dig. He was an engineer, after all.

Sebastian cracked his knuckles three different ways, then spoke. "Cycling five or six hours a day on tour is a license to gorge. A hundred-and-fifty pound person riding at twelve to thirteen-point-nine miles per hour (a leisurely to moderate effort) burns in the neighborhood of five hundred forty-four calories an hour. This means you can shave off two vanilla milkshakes in one hour huffing over those handlebars." Sebastian paused and smiled, perhaps lost in the thought of those shakes. "And that's just the beginning. A guy like you gets to add some major calories burned for higher body weight and higher average speed."

"It's all muscle, Seb. Let's get that straight."

Sebastian rolled his eyes and continued the dissertation. "You hold what, around eighteen or nineteen miles per hour on an average tour and weigh just under . . ." He sized me up like a practiced tailor would. "Say, two hundred pounds . . . which works out to . . ." He scanned the pages of notes. "Hot damn, one thousand one hundred fifty-two calories burned per hour."

We both had to stop for a moment and contemplate such glorious numbers.

"You sure about those calculations?"

But we'd been on the bikes for enough of our lives to know viscerally the truth inside these numbers. To have it confirmed by science made it worth it to have eaten all those second helpings I'd occasionally contemplated putting back.

"What the hell," Sebastian said, the research bug biting him hard at that moment. "After we find a store, let's do a study. We'll keep journals of our calorie intake over this week and put it to the test."

If anything, we learned that we could eat more than the numbers given to us on paper. But I chalked some of that up to the ever-present rolling hills, generally low-fat foods bordering on a healthy diet, elevation gains, and the fact that the International Date Line happened to be so close to New Zealand.

Sebastian chalked it up to the abundance of empty space between my ears.

"You're just jealous that I can eat an extra hundred calories more than you per hour."

But this was like saying I was a slightly wealthier billionaire than my riding partner. We were both beyond the bounds of nature, somewhere in the telephone book between freaks and sideshow attractions.

Based on my calorie burn, Sebastian decided I had the metabolism of a naked mole rat. If it were available, I could have eaten the following per hour:

OFF-TRAIL BIKING: 2 servings apple pie à la mode or 4 Cliff Bars. (I'll take the pie, please.)

ON-ROAD BICYCLING, 12–13.9 mph: 35 servings of beans. (Beans, beans, the magical fruit . . .)

ON-ROAD BICYCLING, 14–15.9 mph: 4 overstuffed bean-and-cheese burritos. (El beano, El beano, de magical fruita . . .)

ON-ROAD BICYCLING, 16–19 mph: That's a complete Wendy's meal—Big Classic, french fries, and a Frosty—every hour. I know it's hard to wrap yourself around these numbers but that's 8–10 combo meals a day if I dared. (Of course there's not a health insurance company in the world that would cover me based on that diet.)

ON-ROAD BICYCLING, 20+ mph: a complete steak dinner, a dozen Little Debbie Devils, and fourteen candy bars sticking out of the top of a pound cake.

Basically, at twenty miles per hour or above I became a culinary superhero, an eating machine able to consume more food than I could possibly carry on my bike.

Once we'd been properly fed again, the calorie-counting engineer and I decided, just for kicks, to track some of our other off-the-bike activities:

ONE HOUR OF SEX: (Moderate—How else would someone do it for a full hour?) 93 puny calories =
one 4 oz. serving of bean curd

WRITING: 71 calories per hour = 1 plum

SOLVING MATH EQUATIONS: 83 calories per hour =
4 carrots

I was stunned by the sex finding, but Sebastian pointed out the undeniable law of science that men tend to shun like talk of a real tooth fairy: Most guys spend so much of their waking life thinking about sex that by the time the clothes actually come off, we've been in a whirling frenzy of mental activity for hours, thus making it *feel* like we've done something of marathon proportions.

"I suppose the lesson here, Sebastian, is if you want to look good in bed or holding a calculator or pounding on a keyboard, you'd better keep riding that bike."

Sebastian fixed me with a smug expression. "I always knew it took more calories to do math than English."

"Ah, but does your little program say whether it's for scribbling a grocery list or penning the next great American novel? Are we talking simple subtraction or calculus?"

Sebastian tended to the pot of food boiling over on my little camp stove. By my estimation, there wasn't a fast-food outlet for five hundred miles.

"Doesn't say. Let's eat. By the way, the data show that you earned forty servings of this vegetable stew if you want."

Another rule of thumb we tested for accuracy was that an average rider (at 15 mph) burns about 20 to 25 calories per mile, ON TOP OF whatever they'd normally eat on a non-riding day. Some afternoons I'd count mile markers as we rode and deposit brownies and slices of pizza into a little savings bank in my brain. We were shameless inside our heads . . . and in New Zealand we were also hungry most of the time.

I hated to say good-bye to Sebastian, but he had a real job to get back to in Europe and I had another continent to explore.

"I hear Australia has lots of junk-food stands," Sebastian said, handing me the holy grail: a complete calorie chart printout.

Feeling like a member of a NASA space team, I noted for the record, "If my metabolism changes midtrip or you somehow manipulated the data, I'll be that cover photo in *National Geographic* of the four-hundred-pound Yank encircled by dingos."

Sebastian flashed the four-finger Vulcan peace hand symbol and said by way of parting, "Eat well and prosper, my friend."

━━■━━

Even when you can locate fast food, dealing with drive-through service anywhere on a bike is tricky business. It was nearly ten o'clock at night in British Columbia, and Burger King was the *only* food choice for miles. The guy who got to wear the manager badge that evening would not, I mean refused, to serve me. Even after I did my best song and dance, he tossed some bogus insurance liabilities issue at me. Only the drive-through was open, so unless I won over this frowning gent, I was out of luck.

Dumbfounded by the corporate logic of it all, I tried reason, I tried a bit of indignation, and then I tried pity.

That was what really stuck in my throat. *Pathetic* doesn't even cover how it feels to nearly be begging for a crappy burger late on a summer evening.

"What happened to all the Canadian charm and hospitality I've grown so fond of during my travels?" I asked.

"I'm from Tacoma," the guy said. And doing the hometown proud this far north of the border.

I thought about it for a while.

"You mean if I got into a car, you would serve me?" I finally asked.

"Uh, yeah, I guess I'd have to." He looked smug. "But we don't get customers this late. So wait all you want." He gave a wicked chuckle as he slammed the window closed.

I pedaled twenty yards away so I could think it through and fume in the darkness. Tired from a long day's ride, I stood over my handlebars in the parking lot. It was my own fault for not planning ahead, but that was the central thesis of my adventures. If you overplan a trip, you reduce its thrill and depth. I suppose some shopping at a grocery store during daylight wouldn't be misconstrued as anal-retentive, though. Nonetheless, I couldn't let one punk rain on a perfectly good travel premise.

This little strip of stores miles from the city was the only sign of civilization, and I was too hungry to give up. Besides, all I had was a tiny bag of corn nuts and some Sweet 'n Low.

Then, like a pimply-faced fairy godfather, the other guy working in the Burger King kicked open the back door to haul out some trash. He eyed me standing over my loaded bike in the shadows. I was ready for more abuse.

"My manager's a real prick, eh?"

"Don't I know it," was my response.

"He couldn't get in the army, so now he hates every-thing."

"You Canadian?"

"Until they pry the last maple leaf out of my cold, dead hands."

We laughed. Now here was a guy I could work with.

"Where you from?" he asked.

"Not Tacoma."

Then I hit upon an idea. Just to be safe, though, I questioned if the manager carried firearms.

"If the army wouldn't let him, Canada sure won't."

When we pulled up to the drive-through window in my new pal's car, the manager nearly blew a gasket. "What the hell do you think you're doing?" he snarled at his fellow employee.

I've never seen a bigger smile.

"I'm on my break, remember?"

Then I leaned over. "And I'm on bag patrol. Would you kindly hand me that order?"

The guy was forced to take my money. And once I had possession of my hot, greasy bag of delight, I stepped out of the car, winked at the driver, and pedaled into the night, my faith in the Canadian sense of fair play restored.

What I learned that night as I hunkered down in the dark along a lonely back road is that fast food is horrible stuff, born out of the bowels of our car culture and this need for insane abundance and immediate gratification. Deep down we all know it. The problem is, those Frostys aren't bad, and as Sebastian helped me quantify, it takes a lot of fuel to keep a bicycle rolling along. Sometimes bankrupt calories are all that's on the menu. But I can tell you this much: Fast-food mediocrity tastes a damn sight better in Canada when wrapped inside a bit of petty revenge.

━━■━■━━

Of course, it helps to be smarter than the food you're waiting for. In Mexico I sat patiently in the saddle of the bicycle, the midday sun at full tilt baking my head through the helmet like a poached egg. Around the twenty-minute mark it dawned on me that the car in front of my wheel had not, in fact, moved an inch. Using my honed-to-barbed-wire-sharpness skills of observation, I determined that it was never going to roll again, or at least not until someone took it off blocks and added four working tires to the equation. What I wouldn't pay for a photo of myself poised there behind that dusty station wagon with U.S. plates, the relic of a summer vacation gone horribly wrong south of the border. The bumper sticker read Hasta La Vista. Not anytime soon was my guess. The photo would include a little arrow pointing toward myself, with the caption "America's best and brightest on vacation." The car ahead of the wagon had wheels, but further inspection showed no hood or motor. A nice prickly pear cactus was working its way up the radiator.

Turns out the drive-through had officially become a walk-through years before. There were more customers on foot than in vehicles to begin with. Also, as evidenced, cars in that town had a tendency to stall or die outright while idling on line. And, due to the less-than-stringent restrictions on lead in gas, some customers gulped down enough fumes with their fries to grow so punchy during their lunch break that they could no longer operate heavy equipment. But these folks were not nearly as dumb as I felt waiting for a cheeseburger that would never come. I wandered up to the window and was rewarded to find cold beer, a popular beverage choice, and many of the customers lounging around the window to drink, nibble at fries, and chat. If any of them had seen me waiting back there like an idiot, well, they didn't let on. Some guy was selling glass vases instead of the Happy Meal toys, and after buying a beer from a tattered cooler below the window, I was given three detailed recommendations and one fairly comprehensible set of directions to authentic, open-fire-cooked tamales. Back at corporate headquarters, Mayor McCheese had to be going ballistic over the dismal food totals at this outlet.

The tamales down the street took a mite longer to prepare, but I had a front-row seat in the shade and savored every damn bite. I vowed to eat only local cuisine from then on—fish tacos in Baja, kangaroo in Alice Springs, and doorstep sandwiches in Ireland. When I backslide these days, it's for a little snack or the occasional Frosty. Hey, I'm only human.

Ride global and eat local. Trust me, it's the only way your stomach's going to respect you in the morning out there on the road.

FOLLOW THE
BOUNCING BALL

It could be that you're in search of a solid anchor, an immovable chunk of truth to help plant yourself in the real world.

Believe me, then, when I say that the best Ping-Pong player on this planet will never make the cover of *Sports Illustrated*. It just won't happen. Nor will you see sexy girls throwing colorful undergarments over that little green-and-white nylon net at the end of a long volley, or rowdy fans in the cheap seats howling profanities at the line judge after a close call. Not a chance. And, as for footage of Gatorade poured over the winning racket hound's coach, well, it does not exist. Not in this universe, anyway. And what of the holy trinity of shoemakers, Nike, Reebok, and Adidas? Let's give up on the thought of them holding patiently on the other end of the phone while a fat endorsement package hangs in the balance.

You want fame and fortune through sport in America? Put on shoulder pads or learn how to shoot from the key. But for whirling hand-to-ball combat, a symphony of intensity, exuberance, manic speed, and stop-on-a-dime agility, for controlled chaos in tight spaces, Ping-Pong has no equal. It's the athletic equivalent of crack. The only reason white mice run on those little wheels is because lab techs won't provide them with tiny Ping-Pong tables and thimble-size rackets.

Much like riding a loaded bicycle around the globe, Ping-Pong is one of those wonderful activities born to lead an underrated existence. It's a character actor in a country that worships movie stars. Throughout many parts of the world the game is cheered, applauded, even revered. You couldn't send the reigning champion of China, Korea, or several equatorial countries walking down the street for fear he'd be mobbed as if he were the fifth Beatle or the second coming of Jesus.

Sitting on a porch outside a ramshackle back-country ranch in Venezuela, I asked a Cuban boy named Ellery, a sweating diamond in the rough, a hidden star of the short table, why he played the game with such devil-may-care fervor. His answer arrived in astoundingly clear and precise English.

"Youth . . . should be a participation sport."

Ellery couldn't have been a day over twelve. He always led with a hard smile across unblemished cheeks and the fastest stroke in that hemisphere—which for my money included both communist and democratic nations. He worked me over like I was a cocky flyweight who'd stumbled into the heavyweight ring by mistake. Armed with short serves, long, fast strokes, and more spin than a whirling dervish, Ellery had any number of ways of punishing those who would take up blades against him.

"Youth should be a participation sport."

What Nike could do with such a slogan. Ellery wore the

remnants of sandals that had to be hand-me-downs from one of the twelve apostles. Apparently Nike hadn't set up shop that deep in Venezuela yet.

Not matter how hard I focused, Ellery continued wiping the table with my game. Hadn't I been the Parks and Recreation Department champion two summers running back in junior high school? Here I was a pure amateur. Once I'd gotten over the shock, though, I considered it something of an honor. The boy's play was flawless, and this from a body that hadn't really even ramped up its testosterone production yet. He was an artist of improvisation, a baron of the blade; it seemed as if I were competing against smoke and shadows. He was barely there one second, then the ball would come rocketing back over the net from an impossible angle.

We were hanging out after a morning at the tables when Ellery lit up a hand-rolled cigarette and whispered, "I want the Korean—Young Fung Choy."

It reminded me of that moment in a noir thriller when someone gives voice and name to an elusive killer who's never actually been seen. Keyser Soze in the film *The Usual Suspects* comes to mind. Ellery took an adept drag off his sweet-smelling butt as though he'd been smoking since around preschool. "They say he was here last week, but that's a lie. I know he's playing the tables in Brazil right now. Word got to him that I want a match, so he might come through before he heads off the continent." Ellery rubbed his eyes, then stared up at the sun, maybe dreaming of the day he and his rival would spar.

"Nobody around here can touch me. Still, they don't

think I have a chance." His hard smile tightened as he stubbed out the cigarette.

"What do you think?" I asked.

"Come on, you want to play some more?"

Any idiot could see I was in for an afternoon of defeats, if not outright frustration. But what a rush to be a sparring partner to this prodigy, and if I hung around a while longer, maybe I'd get to be the corner man in what could be a clash of table tennis titans. A thrill match played off the books and out of the limelight of ESPN and ABC Sports. Anonymous gladiators slashing it back and forth for the sake of struggle, sweat, and desire. In short, the essence of pure sport, the way the Greeks envisioned it, stripped of the modern-day marketing circus.

El Gaucho Ping-Pong in the outback of Venezuela.

And how exactly had I gotten here? Beats me. I remember feeling too cold on my bicycle, so I'd pointed it south months before and just kept pedaling.

To answer Ellery's question, though, I picked up my paddle. "Hell, yes, I want to play some more." I took a position across the net and let the Cuban's game sink deeper into me until the shadows grew long across the room of tables. My arms threatened to go limp. My eyes blurred. And still we battled for the net shots and the long balls that brushed the back edge of the table before slipping out of sight and beyond reach. Only hunger tore us away from the game.

I'd stumbled upon this place while looking for plantain trees. The whole compound was a cross between a secret international training center for Ping-Pong players and a chinchilla ranch. A *Boys of Brazil*–type experiment quietly building a master race of Ping-Pong players with perfect serves and the wrist strength of ten men . . . and chinchillas being raised for profit. Part summer sports camp and part working ranch, no signs promoted its existence and it wasn't on any brochure I could find, but then many parts of South America have a history of protecting privacy. It will forever be a refuge where people, bad, good, or indifferent, come to get lost. Hell, I'd managed to become fairly misplaced without really trying. A great many things seemed to have been left out of the guidebooks for this continent—the good stuff, anyway. But then my definition of good stuff would send the average frequent flying vacationer running for cover and whimpering for room service: festivals in the seedy part of any city, harvesting coffee beans along the thin air slopes of a mountain, hoping logs arranged to form a makeshift bridge over a rain-swollen river would hold long enough to get your loaded bike to the other side. The truth is, I hadn't done much more than pick up road maps at each border and gleam a few vital stats from an outdated Frommer's guide while having breakfast at a youth hostel in Caracas. My standard operating procedure is to make note of the tourist attractions, then avoid as many as possible. Beyond that, surprise me.

After dinner Ellery repeatedly snapped my head back with blistering cross-court returns. *Note to self: Cuban boy should be deprived of protein for many hours, perhaps days, if I am to have any hope of beating him.*

It must have been the slow season, because aside from Ellery and myself there couldn't have been more than a dozen players on the grounds. The Ping-Pong ranch was a casually maintained hideout complete with cheap rooms, spartan and clean, along with simple and equally cheap meals and piped-in music that ranged from Spanish guitars to West Coast surf rock, daddy-O jams from the early sixties. Maybe the sparse number of guests on-site explained why Ellery was honoring me with so much court time. He actually worked at the facility, but I hadn't seen him do anything but play Ping-Pong.

Eventually I had to ask. "We both know there are better players here. I've seen their games. So why do you keep pounding the table with me?"

We were outside. Ellery walked over to my bicycle. He tried to lift it with one hand but failed. After that he banged on the seat and gently kicked the front tire. "You rode this bike all over the world? And from America through Mexico and then all the way to here from Caracas?" It sounded more impressive with a Cuban accent.

"I haven't been paying that much attention to maps, but yeah, aside from a few boat rides over nasty river crossings . . ."

Ellery shrugged and nodded. "That's why I play you."

Whatever Ellery's reasons for our partnership, by the end of the week I was fielding some of the best Ping-Pong of my life. Ellery would lift his grin just a notch when I'd get two consecutive scores past him, at which point his paddle would move with such velocity it resembled the propeller of an outboard motor. I'd brace for impact and keep playing through the barrage as best as I could. But even to be right there with him for a volley or two . . . it tasted like an Olympic moment.

"Can you teach me how to ride a bike?"

I hadn't seen that coming. Cuba has more bicycles per capita than any other place on earth, including China. A buddy of mine made a tour of the country on his own wheels and discovered that after the fall of the Soviet Union, Cuba went from a petroleum-based society to a pedal-powered nation faster than its inhabitants could hand-roll a good cigar. The streets of Havana are one massive group bike ride almost any hour of the day, and the parking lots are stacked and lined with bikes—most of them the Flying Pigeon brand, held together for the most part with prayers and chicken wire. I said as much to Ellery. He confirmed the image my pal had painted of the place.

"But I was so busy playing Ping-Pong, I never learned to ride."

Fair enough. He must have been handed a paddle right out of the womb. But it was the least I could do. So we rambled along the dusty paths of the ranch learning to ride while waiting for this mysterious Korean player whose name reminded me of take-out dinners I ordered a couple times a week when I was back in college.

At first I put him on the seat with me, to give Ellery a clean taste of what it should feel like when he had the balance and speed just right. We resembled the scene out of *Butch Cassidy and the Sundance Kid* where Paul Newman's Butch teaches his lady friend to ride. I felt a little ridiculous pedaling a Cuban teen around the grounds of a chinchilla ranch in Venezuela, but I got over it in a hurry. To mentor another person into a lifetime of pedal pushing was the rarest of treats.

Ellery only crashed half a dozen times—once in spectacular slow-motion fashion—on his way to cycling nirvana.

"Lean back, lean back, *noooo!* Okay, check your serving hand for any damage."

By day's end you'd have thought me a proud parent cheering on my firstborn—in this case my first Communist Ping-Pong player born into the boundless release that is cycling. And he'd done it all in ratty sandals and cutoff shorts on a bike three times too big for his frame.

With the heaps of overly specialized gear—gloves, shoes, and biking jerseys—most cyclists realize that every day on the road is Halloween. Plain and simple, it's wearing a costume each time out of the gate. I've heard bicycle clothing described as the aftermath of a nasty accident over at the Crayola factory, Christmas tree ornaments designed by tripped-out elves after they'd followed the Grateful Dead for a summer, and something a rodeo clown might wear to attract bulls with bad vision. My favorite, though, has to be this one: the love child of a flashy hooker who spent a memorable evening with a tube of kid's toothpaste.

It's all true. We're neon signs, stylistically impaired wonders blinding pedestrians and fooling small children into thinking that the circus has come back to town. As a subculture, we're certainly in no danger of making Mr. Blackwell's annual best-dressed list. I asked Ellery if he'd like the gift of a bike jersey to mark his entry into the world of the wheel.

"Is that a pink seagull flying over a teal mountain?" he asked.

I held up the jersey, abstract art running wild across it.

"Couldn't tell you. But think of it this way," I said. "If you're stranded on an island someday, you can use it to attract search planes."

Ellery thought about this for a moment. "I *was* stranded on an island most of my life, but I don't think that shirt would have saved me."

Point taken. Fidel doesn't have much use for flashy advertising or bright colors. He favors basic greens, desert browns, and no logos of any sort.

Ellery neglected our after-dinner game to pedal and coast the loop around the ranch. He didn't stop until the shadows bled into darkness and the riding became outright treacherous. I corralled the bike for the night as Ellery marveled over how much it felt like flying. He was hooked.

Young Fung Choy strolled onto the ranch the very next afternoon. No fanfare, no press releases, just a rail-thin man, prone to squinting, with a face that, depending on where you stood in the room, looked like either a hungry owl or a predatory hawk. He wore completely nondescript bleached whites—shorts, shirt, socks, and shoes. I wasn't one to tell anybody how to dress, but that attire seemed wrong on so many levels. Wrong anywhere outside of a prim country club, but especially misbegotten for the dusty ranch landscape he found himself in at the moment.

Since Ellery was off creating a childhood memory, experiencing the wind in his face at high speeds during a brief pedal to the river and back, I approached Young Fung Choy first. I think I did so with a bit too much enthusiasm because he recoiled, taking several quick steps back as I rushed the man, a raised paddle in my hand. Who wouldn't flinch when a two-hundred-pound white man, a foot and a half taller, dressed in colorful Lycra, makes a beeline across a nearly empty room for a diminutive guy sporting the hips of a ten-year-old? Hell, I'd have scared myself in that situation. But I couldn't allow this titan of the table to get away. The match meant so much to Ellery. By then it had become something paramount to me as well.

I heard the sound of my freewheel spinning to a stop. Every long-distance cyclist knows the buzz and whirl of his freewheel more clearly sometimes than his own voice.

Once the game had been set up I thought of myself as the local Ping-Pong pimp. We nodded and smiled while waiting for Ellery to gather himself. I might have even thrown in a bow or two. It never ceases to amaze me what an idiot I can be in any hemisphere.

They got right down to business. The wheels on my bike were still smoking when the first serve darted across the table. Young Fung Choy's angry face didn't impress Ellery, and while that outfit might have thrown lesser opponents off track, causing them to lose the little white ball in motion against a solid white background, my paddle-swinging pal was undisturbed. His play was a laser beam of focused energy, all form and execution. Pride swelled up inside me. With Ellery ahead by four points coming down the home stretch, I even tried to start the wave. Something to remember if you ever find yourself on a secret South American Ping-Pong training ranch at the height of a pressure match: Starting the wave is about as popular as passing gas in an elevator. By my third attempt I just looked ridiculous, bordering on unstable.

And then it was over.

I thought they'd play the best of seven, or go for sets like in tennis, but after his decisive win, Ellery simply held the ball down with his paddle, took one more penetrating look at his opponent, then waved Young off. Like any good corner man, I went in close to have a chat.

"What seems to be the problem here, mate?" Sometimes, especially in sport settings, I slip into the lexicon of an Australian rugby player, though I was born and raised for the first half of my childhood in Pittsburgh. Go figure. Maybe too many miles pedaled in the outback. "Everyone knows one game proves nothing. It's a full set or it's really not a fair fight, mate. Now let's have a bash at him."

But Ellery would offer only a pained smile before leaving the table. I heard the screen door bounce closed behind him while I maintained eye contact with a somewhat bewildered Young Fung Choy. A part of me believed that if I just held Choy's gaze long enough, Ellery would saunter back in and play would resume.

I found my Cuban pal riding in circles on the back road behind the estate, kicking up dust in the heat of the day.

"Why?"

He came to a stop inches from me. I gripped the handlebars so he couldn't get away this time.

"That isn't Young Fung Choy," he whispered.

"What are you talking about?"

Ellery shook his head. A deep sigh followed. "Young Fung Choy would never bring such a weak game to the table. I think that's a decoy in there. Maybe he was sent to spy on me. To report back to Choy about potential threats for the future. I don't know what's going on, but I won't rest my game until I play the real Young Fung Choy."

So there it was. Rather than admit his unparalleled skills at the table, Ellery chose to harbor the myth of his unworthiness. Why? Could it be that after admitting he'd beaten one of the best in the world, he'd have to lay down the paddle and find something else to do with his days? He'd still be working for nearly nothing at a guest ranch with a room full of Ping-Pong tables.

"Tell me again why you can't go pro."

"Money."

Ellery was a Cuban refugee living in near poverty with distant relatives in Venezuela. No matter how good he was, to the people who sponsor sanctioned events he was undocumented, invisible. I could see how lack of resources might hamper a dream. He was a boy without a country, essentially. Ellery became my object lesson regarding the rather slim line between dreams and torturous days of desire. I could feel Ellery's unrequited ambition like it was a box of poorly packed nitroglycerine.

"The only way would be for me to go back to Cuba." This time when Ellery smiled it was burnt around the edges. "That I won't do. So . . ." He nodded. "I wait and play, and one day maybe the real Young Fung Choy or some other top player might show up. What else do I have to do?"

At sunrise the next morning, Ellery walked beside me to the road at the edge of the ranch. As I pedaled away from the gate, he jogged along, and when I picked up speed Ellery ran as fast as his legs would carry him, concentrating until exhaustion finally won that volley and took him to the ground.

At least I'd shared with Ellery the thrill of learning to ride a bike. He'd need more than that, of course, but I wanted to believe it was something. It was a start.

Ellery was still waving when I rounded the bend. A Ping-Pong paddle danced back and forth high over his head, and my only thought was of a shipwrecked survivor in a bike jersey, trying his best to be seen.

GETTING INTO COLD WATER

Left arm, right arm, left arm, right arm . . .

It takes practice, and no small measure of luck, to find your rhythm right off. Left arm, right arm, left arm, right . . . breathe.

When the water's cold, as it was that morning just beyond the breakers off New Zealand's North Island, a rookie mistake would be to knife the rolling current hard, discounting form for speed. It's only natural, the body demanding, *Warm me up or get me the hell out!* But like a coked-up drummer in a thrasher band who tries adjusting on the fly to a bizarre request for a Perry Como tune, I went out way too fast, then reeled it in and prayed that no one noticed . . . least of all my own body.

Left arm, right arm, left arm, right arm . . .

The pack comprised a dozen swimmers keeping time and company in the waves around me. These fit young men and women had everything to prove. All but one of us was actually testing to qualify as guards for Surf Life Saving New Zealand. With about eighty clubs dotting the coasts and a rich history of rescue and patrol dating back to shortly after the turn of the century, it's one highly respected organization. Translation: Not just anyone capable of staying afloat for a few minutes without the aid of water wings gets to join the team. Full of good-natured hard bodies willing to pour you a spot of tea and not simply give but enthusiastically rip the shirts right off their muscled backs if you have need of one, these friendly Kiwis thought nothing of gleefully running potential recruits through an aerobic gauntlet of torment and a circuit of cerebral suffering. Here's one telling statistic: A bona fide water rescue or two is often performed on test days.

Since I was not a citizen of New Zealand, my presence in the water was purely recreational, not to mention a rare breed of insanity. As with most of my errors in judgment, this one took place after I'd climbed out of the saddle, parked my bike, and bellied up to the bar. It was more of a beachfront patio than a traditional drinking establishment, but alcohol was distributed nonetheless.

Patrons of the open-air pub bought me a drink on account of I'd pedaled a loaded bike countless miles to their sandy doorstep. I've found that touring long distances on two wheels is similar to being a woman on a slow weeknight in any singles club in the world—men want to buy you a drink and listen to your story whether you want to tell it or not. You're a rolling roadside attraction. I've learned to deal with it. Actually, I enjoy the attention, but it does get me into trouble from time to time.

During this particular conversation, I might have let slip that I'd done some surfside guarding back in the States. Polite but underwhelmed by my declaration, these seasoned pros had surely heard Yanks talking themselves up

on a regular basis. As Americans, we have little appreciation for the John Wayne rep we've collectively established
in minds and hearts around the globe. Not long before meeting the guards, I'd been approached by some Kiwis who
asked to see my gun.

"Excuse me?"

"Don't play coy—you have a large-caliber handgun on
your person. Americans always pack heat."

There had been not a trace of irony or sarcasm in the
young man's voice. His friends had nodded, waiting for me
to produce the goods: a sturdy Glock with laser sighting or,
at the very least, a Saturday-night special with the serial
numbers filed off. Charlton Heston would have been so
proud—choked up is my guess—he'd have saluted those
Kiwi teens on the spot. It seems that reruns of *Baretta, T. J.
Hooker,* and *Magnum P.I.* beamed around the world at all
hours of the day and night have done more for the NRA's
cause than any public service campaign could have hoped
for. We're seen as cartoon characters—Yosemite Sams, plain
and simple—loud, full of ourselves, and ready bordering on
eager to blast our way out of any situation.

Big talk is nothing new from a traveling Yank. But while
I had no NRA card, I did keep my Red Cross lifeguard certi-
fication tucked somewhere inside my wallet (don't ask me
why), and I wasn't shy about flashing it to my guarding
peers at the first possible opportunity. With my credentials
firmly established, that pack of lifesavers made room for another chair around their table. We talked shop, surveyed my
bike, traded stories, and as the shadows grew, I might have
floated the idea that my country's fitness and qualifying
tests sounded slightly more formidable than New Zealand's.

Whatever I professed, and I don't remember the specifics at that point in the evening, my bravado landed me in cold water the next morning, representing God, country, and the whole of the American Red Cross system.

It's an overrated honor to move from anonymous traveler to visiting ambassador of *Baywatch*. My new title carried with it the burden of demonstrating to these buoyant island lads just how well we Yanks can blanket a beach. I remember spouting something the previous evening on the order of "Gentlemen, it's all about whip-smart skill and mongoose speed." But now, a hundred yards into the swim, my overriding goal was simply not to become the lifeless prop in another open-water test day rescue.

———————

Left arm, right arm, left arm, right arm . . .

On a distant shore, years earlier and half a world away, I actually took and passed that open-water lifeguard test, the one I'd bragged about so fervently in New Zealand. Several omissions did occur during the New Zealand retelling—water temperature and wave size would be innocent enough places to start. H_2O along Florida's Gulf Coast feels like a warm bath much of the year. And unless a squall line or its big brother, a hurricane, is bearing down on shore, the water's surface remains as calm as the Dalai Lama and smoother than a grifter on the con. I'd been guarding pools at summer camps for several summers. Boredom and the disorienting stab of too many chlorine fumes chased me to the water's edge. Truth be told, I'd always envisioned sitting atop the big chair for a season, chatting with nearly naked women while I sported Ray-Bans and blew my whistle at the occasional swimmer drifting too close to the boat lanes. Sure, these goals could have been construed as shallow, the petty dreams of a blockhead, but from my vantage point, where volunteering to help your fellow man meant giving the guy at the gym a spot on the bench press, I saw this beach lifeguard job as damn near an act of national service. Like joining the Coast Guard without all those spit-shined shoes and saluting. I was going into the open-water rescue business, damn it. I was willing to save lives *and* rub Coppertone on the ladies if the job demanded it.

Hank was to administer the endurance and skills test. A thirty-year veteran (of war, of distinguished peacetime military service, or of beach patrol—this I never clearly determined), Hank scared the crap out of me in a traditional drill sergeant way. While speaking, he liked to study a spot several inches above your head. Disconcerting in its own right, but when added to Hank's choice of decibel level, a notch below someone trying to drown out jackhammer work, his approach was both garish and mesmerizing.

I finished strong in the swim but felt a sting of fear when Hank bellowed an order to count thirty, then start sprinting the distance between lifeguard stands. Under each station we were to perform first-aid techniques on a volunteer while answering, in machine-gun-fire succession, life-or-death first-aid questions. Whether our answers killed or healed, we had only moments to suck some more air before hightailing it down to the next stand, sand kicking up Jet Ski style in our wakes. Hank gave no indication of our individual performances, but I felt relatively secure that no one had died from my answers, and that as long as I didn't spew breakfast or black out, I was still in the running, so to speak.

Then came the open-water rescues. Carrying a rope buoy, we were to sprint into the surf, swim out to the victim (Hank), assess the situation, and execute a successful rescue. The victim would be passive or aggressive, dealer's choice. As I approached our wild-eyed vet, he bobbed up and down, lifeless as a cork. I reached around his neck, and that's when all hell broke loose. The water churned like a feeding frenzy I'd marveled over as a child. This had taken place inside the shark tank at Sea World. I can still recall standing at that tourist attraction, ten years old, corn dog in one hand, balloon in the other, stunned mute by the relentless carnage of nature, before my parents calmly steered me toward the more orderly world of the bumper boats.

Hank must have had parents once—people to take care of him, to drag him from the wreckage of potential childhood traumas. My guess? He drummed them out of the corps by kindergarten, or they went deaf from all his shouting and just lost their way home one day.

Back in the water it was not going well. Another instant and I was below the surface, encrusted in the drill sergeant's death grip. When all Red Cross–approved moves failed to free me from what was rapidly becoming a watery grave, I decided to think outside the box and delivered three forceful kicks to Hank's family jewels. This unorthodox technique sent my attacker into a fetal position. After hungrily gobbling up some oxygen, I grabbed Hank by the small hairs, performing an actual rescue on one subdued dude. Maybe the third kick was overkill, but I ask you, who is the master of his own adrenaline?

We did not exchange pleasantries. Disoriented or saving up his strength for my lifeguard court-martial, he clung to the buoy in silence while I scissor-kicked us to shore. Hank told me to release him as we closed in on the breakwater. This turn of events was comparable to crashing the vehicle in driver's education or running over actual pedestrians during a road test.

I was done. Maybe they were hiring at the local kiddie pool.

On the beach we avoided eye contact—standard procedure for him, but in my case a deliberate reaction to my shame. Technically, I'd passed. You could even argue I'd proved my mettle under fire.

I did not get the job on Hank's beach. But in an artful move learned on the battlefield, or possibly just something he cooked up before the swelling in his gonads receded, Hank assigned me to the neighboring beach of his lifelong nemesis, Flashback Bob.

Flashback Bob also responded to the names Uncle Bob, Bobby Boy, Captain, F.B., Coach, and, for reasons beyond understanding or at least coherent explanation, Tito.

It was no surprise that Flashback and Hank would vote different tickets come election time, but it ran deeper than ideology, jewelry selection (Bob's included a gold stud earing and yin-yang necklace, Hank's featured dog tags and a Swiss Army wristwatch), or haircuts (Hank, once a week with his own clippers, no mirror; Bob, a rainbow assortment of hair ties to keep that graying ponytail in check). The problem, as I saw it—and granted, I hadn't known either gentleman very long—was that Hank felt he was losing a battle that Flashback couldn't be bothered to play.

Statistically, Flashback ran a better beach, but data never tell the entire story. Hank's stretch of sand was populated with tourists and children, while Flashback dealt with the sunbathers and wind surfers—a much easier lot. Both places were safe as all get out to spend the day, but when Hank ran the numbers, year after year Flashback's turf had fewer reported injuries. The numbers were so close that Hank had to be the only person who made any sort of distinction. Flashback was fond of saying that if everyone was accounted for, that was all the accounting that mattered. Hank had individual ulcers named after each calendar year that F.B. had manned the stand. I knew this not because I'd noted the empty pints of Pepto-Bismol the drill sergeant arranged neatly behind his desk, but because when the two men spoke, Hank always stared F.B. in the eye.

For Flashback, it was a one-off, a hoot. He stared right back but with a smile and felt that if it wasn't him, it would be something else. "Guys like Hank need a target," he'd assert when asked. The running gag at district meetings, and any other time Hank came around, was for all of us to address Flashback by the military moniker Captain.

I figured Hank sent me to Flashback's beach in hopes that a mild screw-up like myself might muck with the numbers just a little. Not so as to cost anyone life or limb, but just enough for the data to tip in Hank's favor. Maybe this was an unfair statement about Hank's character, but you never witnessed the way that pulsing vein stood at attention just above his temple each time the man marched within a hundred feet of Flashback.

As it turned out, there wasn't time for me to screw things up. A month into the season I leapt at a better offer. A summer camp out in California needed a waterfront manager, and though I was living the dream—spending my

Florida nights with a doe-eyed guard named Cindy and my days tanning evenly while bicycling to and from work—I had to shuffle on down the road. Put the word *California* in front of a young man lifeguarding near his childhood zip code and it wouldn't matter if you added the disclaimer "watching mutants swim around in the cooling ponds of a nuclear power plant" to the job description—you're going to get him to bite.

The day I left my beachfront post for the last time, those Florida boys of spring, summer, *and* fall burned some wood on the beach (a misdemeanor) and popped cans of weak beer (misdemeanor number two) in my honor. Hank even showed me a glimmer of hope by acting like he was covering his crotch as I put out my hand to shake. Flashback gave me a hair scrunchie in case I decided to grow my locks long. It would have been an interesting season, but I was searching for bigger waves and grander adventures on another coast.

━━■━━

Left arm, right arm, left arm, right arm . . .

Even as I turned up my pace, the water temperature along the New Zealand coast seemed to drop in an effort to punish me. My mind went to a photo in a natural-history magazine of penguins seasonally migrating to New Zealand before heading home for Antarctica. Clearly a dangerous direction to let my thoughts wander. Now I was absolutely freezing, practically hallucinating that my fellow swimmers were tuxedo-garbed fish. I needed to go further inside myself if I wanted to keep afloat. It was time to locate the Zen of the swim. But since I've never had an off-the-bike mantra—unless you were to count TV sitcom theme songs and advertising jingles for processed cheese spreads—I had to fall back on another memory of warm water. This one came complete with wine, song, and naked women.

In June 1983 I had a clear and present goal to attain. With my high school years behind me and their memories ignored inside a yearbook I'd patently refused to purchase, nothing stood in the way of pursuing the perfect tan.

By my estimation, I had three fat, juicy months stretching out before me to accomplish this delicate task. Toiling part time for three years after school and on weekends at a self-serve shoe pavilion did provide one upside, a strong work-ethic card to play if my parents dared question my blatant sloth that summer. I'm fairly relentless when faced with a concrete, measurable goal, even if that task is simply lying still for hours in the sunshine.

Chuck Burnett, a pal who fell into my most-likely-to-do-anything category of friends, lived next door to a family with a pool and three months left on their Middle East sabbatical. We headed right for the deep end and stayed put as if we were tenants in a rent-controlled apartment. My siblings went out to make something of themselves that summer: A younger brother was busy learning a trade as a journeyman electrician, while my sister spent prime tanning hours punching a register between semesters at college.

That was one of the longest stretches in my life when I neglected my bicycle. Instead, I set myself adrift in a floating lounge chair, AC/DC blaring "Highway to Hell" over and over as the chlorine soaked deep and dangerous into my pores. At some point I commandeered one of my brother's work belts, removing hammers and other tools from the loops and replacing them with bottles of tanning lotion. I had a morning mixture, a midday application, and an after three o'clock cocoa butter rub. I also wore a spray bottle on each hip, like six-shooters, one containing a blend of purified water and lotion (this was for cooling and touch-up coverage of those tough-to-reach areas) and the other refilled regularly with a grape juice and vodka cocktail.

Somewhere scholars were busy changing the dictionary photo for "horse's ass" to a shot of me sporting that work belt of lotions worn low and proudly across my swim trunks.

This dreamy float through a lazy summer came to an abrupt, noisy end late one night in July. As with many situations that slip hopelessly out of control, it began innocently enough, with underage women, fake IDs, and borrowed transportation. It concluded with naked underage women, someone doing cannonballs off a high dive, and the always sobering phrase "You have the right to remain silent."

We'd been pushing the envelope all day. Cloudy morning weather caused Chuck to take us to a small airport on Davis Island where he'd received his pilot's license. My younger brother had the day off, and once I'd hidden his mutated work belt, he was asked to join us. We rented a four-seater plane, surprisingly affordable at $10 per person. Chuck buzzed us over the water, did stalls at five thousand feet, and basically tempted fate and mocked the ghosts of numerous rock stars, all before breakfast.

With his flying time logged for the day, Chuck produced a menagerie of loose beers pinched over time from his older brother's supply. We would have been perfectly content to sit on the side deck and get stupid until the sun came back out but for the crew of perky girls, Eva, Dawn, and Lisa, who pulled up in an expensive foreign-built car. Why do parents give kids not yet old enough to vote vehicles that cost as much as starter homes? As mayor of Slothville, I was in no position to get righteous. Instead, I took the wheel and we wasted someone else's gas tooling around the suburbs. By lunch we'd retired to a hot tub at Eva's palatial home. Things looked promising until a younger sister speed-dialed a parent and we were commanded over the speaker phone to flee the premises before Momma Bear came home and released the hounds.

"But we drove here in your car," my brother pointed out to Eva. In the chaos that followed, someone forgot to close a passenger door as we pulled out of the garage. Metal twists and bends the same on a BMW as it does on a VW—of this we have solid proof A lesser-known fact is that three athletic teens fueled by fear and beer can force that same metal back into place . . . after a fashion.

"Your mom will never notice," Chuck said consolingly. He forgot to add, "If she's suffering from an advanced case of glaucoma." But it seemed to be enough for our perky gals. I drove as best I could through some serious lip locking with Lisa. The girls pulled away with promises of a sexual rematch after dark. We took up the same positions on the deck as we'd been in hours earlier.

"It's gonna be a great night," I announced.

"Not likely," Chuck said. "We'll be lucky to see them before college graduation."

"What are you talking about? The car? There's insurance for that. It's nothing."

Chuck shook his head. "Not that. When I was changing

out of my wet shorts to go, I tossed a pair of soaking Jockeys against the sliding glass door. As a joke."

No one was laughing. He might as well have thrown a winning lottery ticket out the window of a fast-moving car.

"Those girls will be entering a nunnery by dinnertime," Tim complained.

We mourned our losses over another beer. Then the sun came out and all was forgotten.

At dusk a BMW with a slightly bent door idled in the driveway. Already grounded, the girls had decided to complete the sins they were being punished for.

"We snuck out," they giggled in unison.

Hallelujah. Let's all take a moment to praise the initiative of bored women in their waning years of high school.

"Night swimming," Chuck proclaimed. Every boy in America knows this to be the fastest way to release a girl from the bonds of her clothing. We drove off in search of a pool to raid (Chuck's neighbor's was out since it was too close to his parent's bedroom). We prowled the backstreets, but ended up at a country club because someone could run a tab. Security was very polite when they chased us off the premises. It was ironic, since we were actually allowed to be there, but without a parent to vouch for us, we were sent packing.

Anyway, night swimming is more exciting if you're breaking some rules to get into the place. Scaling the fence at the public pool was clearly a violation, but then they'd forced us to become outlaws, hadn't they?

It didn't take long before everyone was performing cannonballs off the high dive, sans clothing. I chose to wear my shorts on my head as a makeshift bathing cap and a political statement about the transparency of current fashion trends. From my vantage point on the board I could see everything. Chuck and his date were relaxing in the bleachers over tallboys. Tim and his gal were giggling in the shallow end, playing a form of Marco Polo I'd never seen before, and my newfound friend was twirling her top above her head while treading water like she was auditioning for a job at the Moulin Rouge. Ah, for this perfect summer evening to last forever. And I dare say I had achieved the perfect tan.

Hey, I don't remember any of us bringing a flashlight. . . .

It was a little over the top for the officers to hold guns on Chuck and handcuff Tim and his date together, still unclothed, and leave them like that in the back of the cruiser all the way home.

In that instant before the officer told me to remain silent, I gazed down at Lisa, who had not spotted the police yet. A sadness of unmeasurable depth washed over me. She was tossing her bikini bottom onto the still-warm concrete and signaling me to dive. Oh, what might have been. What did come to pass involved locating gainful employment to pay off trespassing fines and finance the first month's rent on my new apartment. By August my tan was uneven at best, but I still held a soft spot in my heart for night swimming . . . always will.

━━━■━■━■━━━

Left arm, right arm, left arm, right arm . . .

Other Kiwi swimmers were making their moves now. I could push no harder and lacked the advantage of knowing how much further I had to swim. Everyone else seemed to find another gear, and they chose that moment to floor it.

My efforts focused on slapping the water with just enough force to create forward motion.

Other memories in water began to rush in. I drifted back to one surreal moment in Mexico. What day of the week it happens to be loses value on an extended bike tour, but sometimes a scene snaps you back into calendar thinking. I rounded a rough spot on a remote Copper Canyon trail and knew in an instant that it was Sunday. Confronting me was a picture of shocking beauty: Robed Catholics—missionaries, no doubt—wading into a pool only feet from a cascading waterfall, Tarahumara Indians in tow. The Indians were covered in ceremonial paints, dried chalky dyes forming circles and patterns that would have made Picasso jealous. And the paints did not come off as their heads were tilted back and the Holy Spirit purified them. Silence but for bodies breaking the pool's surface and the steady beat of the waterfall. What caused this scene to transcend the traditional reverence of a Sunday afternoon ritual, recasting it as a poster for religious tolerance and a celebration of cultures in a shrinking world, was that some of the missionaries had actually shed their own clothes and were back on the bank allowing themselves to be painted by the Tarahumaras. I'm fairly certain you couldn't locate such a program in the official missionary handbook, but odds are good it's an exchange that both parties will remember deep into their lives. I stood there voyeurlike for a long time and felt strangely optimistic for my species.

———

Left arm, right arm, left arm, right arm . . .

Gators overran the serene baptism scene in my mind.

As in alligators near Venus . . . the town of Venus, Florida, that is. I'd been laboring as a counselor at Last Chance Ranch, a tough-love program for kids in big trouble. The idea was that building fences, milking cows, and breathing fresh air would turn these teens away from crack, armed robbery, and the like. I saw very few success stories but noticed a lot of nervous cattle. I led groups of these street-hardened lost boys by mountain bike and horseback through south Florida's swamps and sand hill habitats. The other team leader stopped everyone for a lunch break at Green Lake. It was a swimming marsh the color of strong bourbon. I pointed across the murky water, beyond the cypress knees and Spanish moss, to where a dozen hefty gators lounged on the far banks. No one paid attention. Boys dove right into the water and stirred up the muck; a few grabbed canoes that had been left on the bank and started paddling around, throwing sticks and stones at the gators. There was one boy who stayed behind on dry land. He looked like Kid Rock's little brother.

"Why aren't you out there? Can't swim?" I asked.

He waved away a horde of bugs amassing around his stringy, shoulder-length hair. "I can swim like a mother, but I ain't going in there. That crew grew up in Miami. Shit, they think a gator is a mascot for a damn football team."

"And you?"

"I was born out here, man. I don't want no part of that nonsense."

Neither did I.

"You the lifeguard, right? Case these fools need help."

My laughter had real force behind it.

Kid Rock chuckled as well. Like fishermen, we stayed put and waited to see if anything would bite.

———

Left arm, right arm, left arm, right arm . . .

When the swimming got so hard I felt like letting go and sinking like a polished stone to the bottom, I hauled out my wild card memory: the powerful picture of passing a back-yard swim test with Mrs. Robinson. Her last name was ac-tually Pearce or Davenport or something like that, but to me she'll always be Mrs. Robinson.

When I was closing in on thirteen, this rowdy couple moved into the biggest house on our block. They played Donna Summer tunes at all hours, had a tennis court in-stalled, and opened their pool to the neighborhood kids. A sign on the gate depicted a streetlight. If it was green, we could swim, but everyone had to pass a water test first. I missed the group test, so I rescheduled for a solo, early on a Saturday morning.

Mrs. Robinson answered the door wearing nothing but a smile. Hot beyond anything I'd seen in the pages of contra-band magazines, she explained that I was to tread water for fifteen minutes. There was no reference to her lack of cloth-ing. She was all woman, and I was a package of pencil-thin legs, jutting shoulder blades, neck like a giraffe, and excited confusion. Mrs. Robinson explained that she'd keep a timer on me and watch from the bay window while doing some chores. I heard very little of this but managed to wander around to the backyard and slip into the water. As I scissor-kicked about the deep end it felt more like floating through a slightly pornographic version of *Leave It to Beaver.* Mrs. Robinson worked a vacuum, took out the trash, waved to me from the garden, and let me know how much time I had left. No one was going to believe this. Or maybe the other guys knew all about it from their own test day and had sworn themselves to secrecy. One thing was for certain—their pool had the makings of a popular summer hangout. I breezed through my test but was too embarrassed to get out of the pool. I coached myself, *Look away and try to think about anything else . . . the Flintstones, for instance.*

That would be my only swim in their pool. A lawyer who lived down the block informed the couple that they needed permits and handicap ramps to run a public facility. If only we could have gotten that lawyer over for one of Mrs. Robinson's weekend swim tests, the whole thing might have turned out quite differently. It was all for the best, as what boy on the cusp of manhood needed that form of torture? Besides, Reagan was about to take office, and then everyone would be told to put their clothes back on.

■□■□■

Left arm, right arm, left arm, right arm . . .

I was barely hanging on to the surface, but pride wouldn't let me stop, so I sent my mind adrift to a peaceful place, a drowsy summer afternoon on the island of Boca Grande. Circumstances had made me the guest of a distraught college roommate come back home for a long weekend. Kyle was attempting to patch up a dead-on-arrival adult relationship with his childhood sweetheart. I put his chances at success about the same as the planet being taken over by alien Chihuahuas who would make us eat out of plastic bowls in the backyard. But so absorbed was he with winning back the heart of a girl he no longer really knew, Kyle couldn't see that own his parents' marriage was on life support—the disease apparently being booze and money troubles.

I managed to find bliss among the ruins because I wasn't emotionally invested in these people. Kyle didn't seem to like me much—or maybe he simply wasn't too fond of anyone, himself included, at that point in his life. Either way, I was more of a prop so that he didn't have to approach his lost love alone. Given that, I really didn't mind being used. The waters around Boca Grande were decadently warm and the bougainvillea was in full bloom. It played out as I suspected. His heart slashed and pride gone, we picked up bottles of beer at a little store along the canal and bobbed together in a tranquil inlet. I floated without much effort in the salt water, and Kyle had finally stopped talking about himself for a moment. And then the rain began to fall, a light, caressing shower. The rainbow formed almost on top of us. Kyle was the one who spotted it. For a minute or two I actually forgot about having to be an adult for the next fifty years or so.

"You and me have lived together six months, and"—I thought he was going to cry—"I don't even know if you have brothers, or . . ." Kyle's sigh resembled the last bit of air escaping a bike tire. "Am I one big shitheel or what?"

They say identifying the problem is the first step toward a solution. We reintroduced ourselves there in the backwater and, against major odds, ended up legitimate friends by the fall semester. Whenever I think of Kyle or the island of Boca Grande, I catch a faint taste of flowers and feel myself float slightly off the ground.

━━ ▬ ▭ ▬▬

Left arm, right arm, left arm, right arm . . .

It was the last water memory I wanted to have, but I could hold it back no longer. The Tapouni brothers' dad was a captain of the air-conditioning business in Florida, so they did not want for much in life. He put in a black-bottom pool my summer between elementary school and junior high. It was gonna be the next big thing. We spent so much time on their side of the fence that our mail started arriving there.

With a black-bottom design the sun heats the water year round. Late August snuck up on me. I was having abandonment issues: I didn't want to abandon the hard-fought pleasures of comic books, pint-size cartons of milk on school lunch trays, and ruling the playground with casual benevolence. Junior high was about starting over with a new map. I was tired of being a pioneer. Couldn't I just stay at the bottom of that warm, womblike pool forever? Rays of light penetrated the surface but the dark walls wouldn't allow them to reach my home on the bottom. By remaining perfectly still, like a manatee, a person can stay safely submerged for a surprisingly long time. With my eyes open, all was reassuring blackness. Then I heard playful shouting from far above. In came the cannonballs, tight bodies off the diving board crashing my sanctuary. I reacted to get away and slammed my head hard into the side of the pool with enough force to make me see stars. Judging distances, it turns out, is difficult in a black-walled pool—one reason why the product never caught on. The oldest Tapouni brother laid hands on me, and a moment later I was coughing across the patio.

People were willing to buy my explanation, I was willing to buy my explanation, but it occurred to me with disturbing clarity just how unconcerned I'd been for a moment or two there about surfacing.

It was time to embrace junior high.

▬▬▬▬

Left arm, right arm, left arm, right arm . . .

And it was also time to face some facts in the Southern Hemisphere. I stopped swimming and looked around for something in the cold waters of New Zealand that might save me. Let someone else be the ambassador of *Baywatch*. I wanted only to return this borrowed wet suit and participate one more time in my true calling: riding a bicycle, with its familiar pedals, brakes, and shifters . . . and the ability to breathe whenever I damn well felt like it.

The boat was nearly on top of me before I heard the roar of its outboard.

"You overshot the course by nearly a quarter mile." Among my saviors was one of the guards from the previous evening. The teasing was sure to be relentless.

"That's a nice stroke you have, but do the victims on your beach take a number while you eventually home in on them?"

And so it went. I deserved this good-natured abuse and even enjoyed it once I'd stepped on solid ground again. The club awarded me a special honor, a waterproof compass that I was to keep handy during all future rescues—or anywhere I went, for that matter.

As the gang was seeing me off, I leaned over my handlebars, calling them in close. I couldn't resist, knowing that it would be different this time, knowing I could take each and every one of them if they'd just go round up some bicycles and meet me at the top of the hill.

I glanced from face to face, at all these able-bodied gents, smiling, listening, and clearly up for any challenge. That's when a tiny sliver of self-control—maybe it had been lodged behind a molar all these years—broke loose and saved my ass.

"I . . . We should . . . Listen, if you guys are ever in my neck of the woods, stop by and we'll go for a swim, but don't call me for directions."

The group fell apart with laughter.

It was safe to ride away now, the myth or reality of my cycling prowess still intact. Of course, I was not certain how to get back to the main road, but I'd be damned if I was going to ask those boys.

THE SMALLEST CAR
IN IRELAND

Even from my rather poor vantage point twisted deep in the thickets and tangled around my bicycle frame, I could see that she was crying.

Her head moved slowly forward and back, a gentle touching of the steering wheel on the downswing, like one of those dashboard Madonnas you can buy now at the Vatican gift store. Tears began to run the woman's mascara, adding to the Virgin-Mother-weeping-for-our-sins effect. I hopped up in quick fashion, or as rapidly as someone battling thorny brambles and gravity can be expected to, especially one who has just been run off a quaint country road by the Holy Mother.

Part of rural Ireland's charm is those narrow lanes, tight curves, and lush hollows. Hell, there's a reason cars there are the size of refrigerator boxes and most Irishmen can drive with their knees by the time they're knocking on puberty's door. But it doesn't make a touring cyclist's job any easier. To say nothing about the fact that she had been exploring both sides of the road and redlining that little engine like some sort of deranged Shriner moments before she clipped me.

I refused then, and resist now, whining over issues involving other countries and driving on the left side of the road. I bring it up only to point out the simple but crucial need to adapt or perish in this world. Since I hadn't shuffled off this mortal coil at that juncture, or suffered more than a few scratches, I decided to climb out of the ditch and assure the tearful lassie that all was right in my world. The least I could do as a guest in her country.

Single at the time, and therefore lacking the proper training or emotional equipment to deal with a crying woman anywhere, let alone a stranger bawling behind the wheel of an automobile, I bounded over, offered her a toothy smile and a wave just this size of Texas. Friends have dubbed it my St. Bernard approach to life: loud, gregarious, quick with a joke and a story or three. In most parts of the globe I'm spotted right off as a boisterous Yank (decidedly different from an ugly American, except for the noisy part), but in Ireland, if only I could have mastered a decent accent, I'd have been mistaken for one of the lads everywhere I went. Unfortunately, my vocal impersonation of an Irishman is pitiful.

"Imitation might be a keen form of flattery where you come from, but Jaysus, that accent you're attempting is nails on a board, nails on a bloody board. Shut your gob and drink this one on the house."

She took one look at me, grinning there like a fool near the passenger-side window, and burst into a new round of tears.

This was getting serious.

"It's okay, you didn't make solid contact . . . not really. It was more of a nudge." I patted myself down, cop-on-the-beat style, to prove I was in good condition.

With great effort the Holy Mother began to find her calm, and after a few cheek wipes with the back of her hand, the biblical character started to fade, replaced by a woman in her mid-forties with attractive earrings and even the hint of a smile. She leaned across the seat.

"I'm Tracy. Sorry 'bout the nudge and all the water-works, but it's something of a shock . . . with your blond spiky hair you remind me of my son. He's gone now . . . three weeks it will be Monday, and seeing you there was just too much. I'm a fool . . . sorry."

And again the tears started to roll.

Like a bomb squad tech after cutting the wrong wire, I looked around for some sort of split-second inspiration that might save me, as if I could unearth and kiss some distant cousin of the Blarney Stone, a Blarney Pebble maybe, dis-carded along the roadside. It wouldn't give me the unending gift of gab, but all I wanted was a small window in which to utter the perfect words, something to comfort and cheer while not making it worse. Talk of death is such a heavy conversational baton to be handed. It's times like this when one realizes the true worth of a good greeting-card copy-writer. I wanted to say the right thing, but it was at that very moment I caught a look at my back wheel poking out of the bushes.

"Ahhh . . . for Chrissake!"

My outburst came forth with such force, it stunned Tracy into silence. Upon closer inspection, I saw that the wheel was in even worse condition than I'd thought. Silently we put my wounded steed a third of the way into the boot of her car. I strapped it down as best I could, then took a cramped position in the front seat.

"I'm sorry for your loss," I said, wearing a contrite expression—I was going for that understated funeral director gaze.

Surely they'd have kicked me out of greeting-card boot camp before lunch on the first day.

"But I'm sure he's in a better place now." Fantastic—always follow up sophomoric drivel with the lamest of platitudes. But I'd gone that far, so I had to make eye contact. Her look was quite odd for a grieving mother.

"That's doubtful. Unless you think Boston has something over Ireland. Lost my boy to the flash and pan of the States, and we know he won't be jumping back over the pond for what could be years. My sister went to Boston once and says it's more or less bad drivers with funny accents. I have a fool for a son. But then he thinks he's going to make a name for himself playing that punk rock music."

As I strained to make out all the words through her thick accent, I couldn't hide my grin. Hadn't she just run me down with a motor vehicle? This woman would be right at home in Beantown.

She laughed off the last tear, then chided my smile. "Come now, this is serious. And to think I bought that wanker his first U2 album many moons ago. He's taken to calling Bono a two-bit messiah just to annoy me and feels strongly that the ghost of Sid Vicious could kick Bono's ass."

Never let it be said the Irish lack a flair for the dramatic.

I took a moment to picture the lead singer of U2 executing some *Karate Kid*–style moves while a pasty Mr. Vicious snarled and jabbed at him with a dirty hypodermic needle.

"Does your boy have any tattoos yet?" I asked.

"None that he'll show me, but so many piercings that when I was trying to say good-bye, he set off the airport metal detectors worse than a terrorist."

Her son would be fine, but the jury was still out on my situation. I tried to ease back in the minute front seat and, following Tracy's lead, attempted to ignore the speed limit.

A few bumps and twists down the road, she announced that I was in good hands. Tracy knew someone who could sort me out properly.

"He's a mechanic. Best in the county."

All well and good, but I wasn't bringing in a Chevy with a blown valve. Trueing the spokes of a wounded wheel is an art form. Many a car mechanic has learned the hard way that while bicycles have fewer parts, there are precious few a rider can do without. Consider that a car will motor along just fine with a busted air conditioner, a broken taillight, and many other parts on the fritz, but aside from a tweaked bell and maybe some unraveling handlebar tape, cyclists need everything from brake pads to seat posts to links in the chain if they want to remain upright and healthy.

"There's just one thing—don't let him start playing his organ for you."

Now that's advice you don't receive every day.

As Tracy stepped on the gas, I mulled over this obscure and mildly alarming counsel but, as with many of the events of that day, decided just to let it ride.

I hoisted my bike out of Tracy's boot as a well-groomed man nodded from his porch. If this was my mechanic, he'd successfully disguised himself as an accountant. Beside him, a younger, rumpled, and scraggly version of the gentleman—an accounting-school escapee working as a roadie for Aerosmith, maybe—leaned back on two legs of a wooden chair with hands laced behind his head.

"Suffered a little casualty, have we?" the roadie asked, not unkindly. His father used a magazine to swat him forward in the chair, delivering force that was just this side of playful.

"Jaysus, get yourself a dog if you want to slag someone like that!"

But they were smiling. I even heard the roadie bark, border collie style, a few times in his father's direction as he came down off the porch. He took the bike out of my arms like an experienced rider. Someone who doesn't pedal often will hold a frame as if it's a mercy date at a Sadie Hawkins dance: reluctantly, with trepidation, and at arm's length. But the roadie snatched it up with one hand, hoisted it onto his left shoulder, and held it close and steady—a lover on a weekend tryst. I suspected there was a nice Raleigh or Bridgestone on the premises, a bike of some quality that saw regular use.

"That's Billy, and, though the lad loathes to admit it, up there on the porch would be his father, Gerry."

"Oh, Da's above the fray, just misguided."

Gerry nodded.

"And Billy there—he's about as useful as a cigarette lighter on a motorbike."

The two men squatted over my rig and with the light taps, half whispers, and nods of people who have worked and lived together forever, they came to a professional consensus in about ten seconds.

"Billy's going to do the work on this one," Gerry announced.

I knew it.

"Could be a day or two, though. For when I use the term *work,* don't expect a flurry of aerobic activity or deafening sounds of industry. He likes to save most of his strength for quitting time."

"Play hard and . . . play harder," Billy noted with an unapologetic grin.

These two were priceless.

"Send the tally to me," said Tracy.

Again Gerry nodded.

I smiled in Tracy's direction. Considering the amount of litigation it might have taken in a small-claims court back home to get someone to pay for damage to a bicycle—that's if the driver stops at all—Tracy's offer was refreshing.

"But why don't we come up for a bit of tea first?" Billy proposed. For the record, I didn't see Gerry resisting the notion as I vaulted up the steps.

Thus began my rent-free stay at the best damn father-and-son shade-tree garage and impromptu bed-and-breakfast in all of Ireland.

To the chagrin of any card-carrying Audubon Society member, there were dozens of neon-colored bird-shaped piñatas hanging from the rafters of their work area. Ferns were interspersed along the supporting beams. A pleasantly freakish blend of *mercado* and mechanic's garage, the space was in perfect order. No grease or errant car parts tossed about, two clean bays, and every tool in its place. Gerry ran a tight ship, but what the hell was with all the birds? Various breeds and species twirled ever so slightly on nearly invisible strings, toucans and parakeets ready for happy children to beat the living crepe paper out of them at a birthday party or holiday function. Add one of those sounds-of-the-jungle tapes and a bit of humidity and you could rename the place Rain Forest Repairs and Tune-ups.

"You guys running a little party supply biz on the side or is this the famed piñata wildlife refuge I've heard so much about?"

Billy grinned as he placed my rear wheel into a vise. "My da got those birds after Mom took to bed. She always wanted to visit the tropics, always, but when it was clear she had a bad dose and wasn't going to get back up, he ordered dozens of them out of a catalog and hung 'em all over her room. Guilt. Da was the one who'd kept putting their vacations off, and at that point it racked him with regret. After everything was said and done, I didn't have the heart to toss them in the dustbin, and Da didn't have the energy. Plus, even with the exchange rate and all, they weren't cheap."

He was right, these didn't look like dime-store piñatas.

"Da was a wreck, we're talking clinical, so I brought them out here to brighten up the place. I came to enjoy them, but far as Da was concerned, it didn't help much. Nothing helped, really, 'cept maybe time and that organ of his."

Again with the organ?

The organ I'd been warned of turned out to be one of those maroon-colored electronic deals with a host of ambient sounds, programmed melodies, and a built-in drum machine—the sort of instrument that during the 1970s gave mediocre keyboard players like those in Yes and ELO rock-star-size careers—that coupled with solid management, a rash of casual drug use, and a deluge of blacklight posters jamming people's synapses.

In all that time, I'd convinced myself that no one actually purchased mall organs. Such stores, with their retired band teachers and starving piano instructors hired to play overblown versions of "Feelings" in four-part harmony with a programmable trumpet fanfare chaser, had to be fronts for fencing stolen merchandise or some nefarious pyramid scheme, right? But here in the living room of an Irish hill country home was evidence to the contrary.

While Gerry took a seat in front of his impressive machine, which sported a triplex of keyboards, and began throwing switches and twirling knobs as if he were an airline pilot going through his preflight checklist, I recalled an exchange I once had with a Gen-Xer working the counter of an Orange Julius.

"You like that crap?" he asked while mixing my fruit shake. I must have been unconsciously humming along with the organist jamming through an extended dance remix of "Jingle Bells" next door. "Try listening to it all damn day." He nodded, then held out my drink. "Me and that dude over there at the Chick-fil-A are considering something drastic. He plays anything else by Barry Manilow, he's going down." Which only reinforces my belief that anyone old enough to vote should not be allowed to work at the mall.

Gerry's organ appeared ready for takeoff. He leaned forward, smoky piano bar style, and announced his first selection would be by Van Morrison.

I was encouraged.

But Gerry proved an earnestly bad musician. He played like a harried businessman trying to eat something hot while rushing for a bus. All of the precision and restraint I'd observed in his work as a mechanic was now absent, replaced by a wild abandon about everything, tempo and note selection included. It's only a guess, but I think he was attempting to marry the bouncy freedom of Jelly Roll Morton with the rowdy, bad-boy exuberance of Jerry Lee Lewis. That or fight off a good-sized seizure.

When it was over, detectives at the top of their game could not have determined which Van Morrison song had been performed, but considering the musical carnage as a whole, this seemed a minor point. Gerry certainly had a fan in his son, though, who'd been tapping to an undisclosed beat, hooting now and again, and smiling throughout.

"You're too much, Da," Billy said with enthusiasm.

My turn.

Best I could do was nod in agreement. Or nod and let them interpret it as a positive response. It felt like they wanted more, so I added, "You know, they sell these organs in malls all across America . . ."

━━━━━━━━

Over three days of tinkering and tweaking Billy took a wheel that I'd considered ready for the trash heap and trued it into showroom condition. Pulling out his own bicycle, a mint-condition Cannondale, he suggested we roll my wheel through its paces, maybe get some exercise in the bargain. For a long-distance touring cyclist, pedaling along without bags of gear is a liberating, if slightly naked, feeling. You experience a lighter-than-air sensation for a few glorious miles. It's a grace period I try to take full advantage of by going very, very fast. Billy kept up nicely, which let me know he was a stronger rider than me on any given day. We rested at the top of a hill ten miles from the garage.

"You should stick around a day or two. Our parish is having its end-of-summer barbecue tomorrow. Lots of pints on the dole, good food, and live music."

We made eye contact, and he read my snobbish little mind. "Don't worry, Da won't be playing his organ."

I tried to backpedal. "He's really not . . . I mean the guy can . . ." I settled on "He plays the hell out of it from start to finish."

Billy laughed until he choked up some water and I had to smack him on the back a few times.

"Everyone for three counties knows his playing is bleedin' desperate, but you just can't fault something that brings one person that much joy."

"Seemed like you were encouraging him the other day," I said.

"It just sounded like I was," Billy countered. "When I tell him he's too much, I really mean he's too much . . . but that organ is the best medicine on the planet for my da. No need for me to be cruel to be kind. Truth as I see it, there's no finer mechanic for hundreds of miles, but fixing cars is just a job to him. When he gets behind those organ keys, though, he's on top of the world."

It started me thinking about all the open-mic vocalists, stand-up comics, and amateur athletes bringing up the rear but toughing out the course just the same. The irresistible pull toward a passion when it's clear one's talents lie in another direction, imaginary accomplishments, and that oh-so-delicate delusion that every day in every way we're getting better and better . . . say what you will about natural selection and the genetic weeding out of traits that don't serve us well, but I think that somewhere deep down, the powers of the universe who wired us from the get-go . . . well, they love a long shot. That and maybe a good laugh.

And Billy thrilled at seeing his da shine. Armed with this realization, I vowed to be a more charitable critic at certain art gallery openings, college theater productions, and poetry slams. Or, like a giddy Frenchman at a Jerry Lewis film festival, I would embrace the singular energy of the work rather than its potential for greatness.

To this day, though, I draw the line at any music collection with Barry Manilow box sets.

Rain threatened to pelt, pushing the end of the summer social down to the local pub, but an afternoon light snuck its way back around the edges of the horizon and the wind died down. While there was no mistaking the place for spring break at Daytona Beach, Florida, of course I stuck around for the party. If a solo cyclist wandering Ireland, or anywhere else for that matter, isn't willing to act like a human tumbleweed, then the joke's on him. To contort and twist the immortal words of John Lennon, the ride is what happens while you're making other turns . . . coo-coo-ca-choo. Besides, rumor had it the Holy Mother Tracy was whipping up some sort of apple pastry so breathtaking that felons on the run would break stride just for a taste.

Fat, happy, and clasping a pint of plain in one hand and the remains of an apple turnover in the other, I found a spot on the grass and waited for the entertainment to commence—penny whistles, hand drums, those under-sized guitars I can never remember the name of, and a fiddle or two deftly played by a frisky redhead frolicking shoeless to the Celtic beat. Stereotyping? Clearly, but truth be told, I'm always trying to wish a frolicking redhead or two into the mix, be it Irish music, urban hip-hop, or German polkas.

To say I was surprised when the band took their places behind rows of xylophones and two steel drums doesn't begin to describe my state of mind. I'd walked by those instruments a number of times that afternoon, even used the largest of them as an impromptu drink holder, but my brain never made the connection. One of the musicians sported red hair—that was a start. He also displayed solid biceps, a five o'clock shadow, and thick black boots. Hopes for a Celtic session and barefoot nymphs looked dim, but I could shift gears and rally for a bit of that island sound, mon. Good music is a treat no matter where in the world you find yourself.

Then Gerry found a spot behind one of the xylophones and my heart sank further.

Turns out that, unlike the organ, you just can't play a xylophone with too much passion. It takes everything you throw at it and more. All of Gerry's misdirected fervor, so lost on the keyboard, found its mark in the center of those pounding vibrations.

The music really cast a festive spell over the rest of the

day. At one point I climbed to the top of a jungle gym in the side yard and gazed over sprawling fields of green. An emerald moment.

"Be a pal and hoist me up." It was Billy.

The band launched into an inspired version of that King Harvest classic "Dancing in the Moonlight." It hit me in all the right places.

"Quite the hooley," Billy announced, all smiles.

We watched the band, Gerry hammering away with his eyes closed.

"He's decent with those mallets," I remarked.

Billy threw an arm over my shoulder. "Brilliant he is, absolutely brilliant." And the way he said it, I knew he was speaking less about the man's playing than about the gloriously complicated sum of his parts. "But don't tell him I said as much. Bloody organ's enough to deal with."

We laughed into the wind.

Was I that different from Gerry? Competent at any number of things that provided pleasure, but from the moment I could balance on two wheels the bicycle had grabbed my heart. And yes, I harbored dreams of greatness. Even when it was clear that I'd never be a threat to any land speed records, that I was more of a tropical depression than a class five hurricane, that if I wanted a yellow jersey I'd have to buy one at the store like the rest of the mortals, I would not, could not get off my bike.

Instead I rode it in another direction, at my own speed.

And years later, my refusal to quit the road deposited me shoulder to shoulder with Billy, Gerry, and the lot of 'em, rowdy Irishmen banging out a joyful noise across the remains of the day.

We'd pedaled our bikes to the party, Billy and me. I spied them propped casually against the rectory wall—a building older than most any structure back in my own country. It dawned on me that I was a damn long way from home but not a bit homesick. On the contrary, for the first time in ages, I felt truly comfortable in my own skin.

LUNATIC FRINGE:
MAKING THE CASE FOR CYCLING'S PATRON SAINTS

Bicycling is like church—many attend, but few understand.
ANONYMOUS

I was called crazy again, in Canada of all places. This pronouncement came from a few of the more evangelical members of the noncycling public. The driver was slouched over the wheel of a puke-green Nova with noisy headers. A glimpse into his thought pattern might have gone something like this: *Buy Camaro, total Camaro, buy GTO, total GTO . . . rinse, repeat.* His passenger, cigarette dangling, was also a ranking officer of the why-walk-to-the-end-of-the-driveway-when-you-can-drive-there club.

My route took me across a long bridge with no shoulder or sidewalk. Of course it was rush hour. Who wouldn't hold the lane in that situation? Keeping up nicely with the flow and seeing that it was a seventy-foot drop to the water below, I just didn't want to be boxed out and pitched over the side for a final, fatal dip.

I waved off their taunts and choked away the high-octane exhaust, but it started me pondering: At what point does religious fervor for the two-wheeled wonder beneath my legs slip into the danger zone? When am I still a tourist in Crazyville and when do I become a full-blown local? More important, would I be able to tell if the transformation had already occurred?

220

You can clip out any time you want, but you can never leave.

Granted, cycling never merited a choice line in an Eagles song, but it does have the right ring. It expresses a certain sentiment shared by riders from Nova Scotia to the Ho Chi Minh Trail. Once a pedal junkie, always a pedal junkie, even if you haven't sat in the saddle for a while. There's some bedrock truth to the expression "It's like riding a bicycle."

I've heard it said that to create something powerful in this world you have to be a little nuts. And cycling is both powerful and thoroughly misunderstood by a good chunk of the population. People think you're nuts to strap a little piece of Styrofoam to your head and enter traffic atop tubes of metal and wheels of rubber. But what many haven't noticed is that there really is a revolutionary living under their roofs. Sure, it doesn't chant slogans and engage in armed resistance, but it's a force to be reckoned with all the same. It bunks down in the garage or waits patiently in the corner. To most it disguises itself as a child's toy, a deceptively simple device for cruising on the weekends. But in truth, a bicycle is lightning in a top tube, a rebel with a cause just waiting to change your life. It's Gandhi, it's Michael Jordan. Hell, it's Teddy Roosevelt and all of his Rough damn Riders rolled into one fluid work of chrome alloy art.

The bicycle can be a symphony one day and an all-night rave the next. Pedal around for a while and you'll have all the proof you need of a playful God. Stronger than St. John's wort, as powerful as Prozac, and more vibrant than Viagra, the bicycle saves drunks and junkies alike. It's rescued countless couch potatoes from the mushy twilight of a

TV's glow and turned back time for old guys who thought their day was all but done. It rescued me from a dull life before it really began.

And while I wait for the world to discover what some of us already know, I think it's time to name a few patron saints. Everyone needs role models, luminaries to light the way. The strength and comfort that come from overlooked geniuses who will inspire and guide us, either back onto the straight and narrow roads or right over that precarious edge.

NOMINATIONS FOR CYCLING SAINTHOOD

Alfred Jarry The French absurdist poet and playwright couldn't get enough of his ride. Accounts describe him as pedaling around Paris like a madman, refusing to relinquish the road to anything, large or small. Atop his Clement Luxe rig, bought on credit and never paid for, Jarry packed two large *pistolets* that he brandished on a regular basis as a form of intimidation, and because they caused cultured folk to stop, point, and stare. When approaching intersections, he was known to fire those matching guns into the air, and possibly in other directions, to warn off traffic. I suppose a standard horn or bell wouldn't have given a man of his creativity that certain *je ne sais quoi*. The Greeks asked only that a man live with passion. Jarry fit the bill and then some. Sainthood for this fallen angel is in order.

Mark Twain Was spotted on a bicycle of one model or another right up to the end of his days. Several accounts recall the pedaling machine as a regular stowaway aboard the paddleboats he piloted. Now that's having your luggage priorities straight. Certainly Twain's famous quote about getting a bicycle—"You will not regret it—if you live"—that fight song of sorts has inspired more than a few mangy pedaling life forms to give the open road one more shot. But the story that adds weight to consideration for sainthood is that of Twain being able to seemingly disappear around deadlines for those news stories he found particularly repugnant or irrelevant. I'm convinced that the bicycle had much to do with his quick escapes. It was easy enough to find him, though, holding court in his dapper white suit at a local saloon. If not bestowing sainthood, I'd like to bring the old dodger back from the dead and put him in a lively bar over in purgatory for a round or two and a few of his clever one-liners.

Queen Lead singer Freddie Mercury deserves sainthood just on the strength of his cycling anthem "Fat Bottomed Girls." No one did more to get people off their arses and into the saddle than the man who penned the opening words, "I want to ride my bicycle, I want to ride it where I like!" True story: My buds and I would pedal the cul-de-sacs of Florida's suburbia in search of pop bottles and prepubescent girls in training bras squandering their summer vacation on trips to the mall. Before Walkmans dominated the landscape, John Greene strapped a boom box to the handlebars of his Mongoose and we'd troll behind them, blaring the Freddie Mercury classic. Our musically referenced worship of their backsides fell on deaf ears. They probably thought we were making fun of those nubile bums. You'd be surprised how fast girls can run in beach sandals when Queen is chasing them. But the summer wasn't a total loss—right before my pop told me to turn that crap down or I was grounded, he commented, "The man does sound like he's had some formal voice training."

Brother Timothy McCleary Rides from his Irish cottage behind the rectory to the corner pub every afternoon, rain or shine—more often rain. When I met him, Brother Timothy was blind in one eye and kept a full-grown collie in a wire basket across the front of his rig. It was the dog's job to bark when our man of the cloth headed for a ditch or the back end of a parked car. The loyal animal also alerted pedestrians and drivers alike that Brother Tim was on the move. Members of both the church and the pub congregations claim to have seen the collie perched in Timothy's lap late one evening, assisting with the steering process, as Timothy sang incoherently in a beautiful baritone. But these gentlemen admit to consuming a pint or two themselves that night, so they couldn't be sure. The only certainty is that Timothy was at his pulpit bright and early that Sunday morning, his trusty three-speed, still in one piece, parked alongside the chapel door. God protects the brave and foolish, but a damn smart collie never hurts. How about we buy Timothy a pint and give the collie cycling sainthood?

Barbara Savage Author of *Miles from Nowhere*. The first person to bring it back alive and kicking for the rest of us. A bull-headed woman with scant cycling experience who decided to get on one and see if it could usher her around the globe. It did that and more. The ride broke her, put her back together, and transformed what would be the final days of Savage's life into a symphony of pain, euphoria, and accomplishment. How do we know this? Because Barbara had the courtesy and foresight to write it all down. It's the cyclist's bible. She bitched and moaned and saw it through familiar eyes, wrestling a relationship, self-doubt, and fear of strange lands, customs, and foods into a worldview as she pedaled all the way home.

The Wright Brothers Was it a stroke of genius to strap those first wings onto a bicycle or simply the mother of invention? Regardless, it burns in the mind's eye that we would not have reached the heavens without those wheels and chain rings and . . . have you ever tried closing your eyes on a fast descent at night? Not for long, just enough to really feel like you're flying. Then hold the tuck a moment or three longer. It's harder to do than you'd think. Forget meditation, group therapy, and expensive treatments. If you live, there are few feelings like it. I bet Orville and Wilbur closed their eyes just a little on those first flights. Sainthood for the boys—an open-and-shut case.

Einstein It is widely documented in print and on Kodachrome that the wild man of physics came up with the theory of relativity while atop his bicycle. Enough said. He gets sainthood for that alone, but the hairdo also proves Big Al was one of us. That was helmet head to the tenth power.

Eugène Christophe The pedaling equivalent of a Special Forces soldier. This guy would be captain of the All-Madden Team if there were such a thing for cycling. His Tour de France resumé reads like that of a war correspondent. Christophe broke his fork in 1913 on the Tourmalet, again in 1919 on the cobbles in northern France, and—I kid you not—a third time in 1922 on the Galibier. In 1913 he was fighting for the lead, and in 1919 and 1922 he was in the lead and lost the race because of the forks. He was also the first ever to wear the yellow jersey when it was introduced in 1919, survived the fighting in World War I (which racer Octave Lapize and others did not), and had his name emblazoned on toe straps like Binda. He was still racing at age thirty-eight. His own rig in ruins, he borrowed a bike from a spectator and chased down the leaders (who were, by this point, nearly an hour ahead) in eight inches of snow on the Turchino climb to take a stage win. Either he made a deal with the devil early on or he was some sort of cycling saint from day one and managed to hide his wings under his jersey.

Lance Armstrong He's such an obvious choice for sainthood that I expect grief for including him, but frankly, my dear, I don't give a damn. Some moments in life can't be explained by science. Let's look at Mr. Armstrong's stats. Cocky contender, check. Cancer survivor, check. Tour de France record-smashing victor, check. Living to see his children born and growing up, check. Hammering a third yellow jersey across the finish line to prove it wasn't a fluke or a short reign, check. All these are overwhelming reasons for sainthood, but when Lance discovered that the bicycle was not only the perfect tool for winning races but a friend that could transport him away from time and place—that the ride, my friends, is the thing—well, he closed a circle for me and I expect, many others.

There are many more out there, rolling their way into your heart, keeping you from taking the car to work, the store, or school when the weather turns a bit sour, and reminding you to cherish what it feels like to fly, skate, and shimmer over the earth on these magical contraptions.

The next time you realize you are in fact a spandex freak, a pannier-packing outsider, a metal-moving minority on the edge of the world, just remember that you're in damn good company.

CONFESSIONS OF
A KILT-WEARING COWBOY

Sunburnt, windblown, half mad from the heat and the sounds of my own exertions, parched, pocked with welts from various and sundry insects, covered from head to toe in a dusty veil of outback crimson, I had only the strength left to witness the sun bury its shimmering tail gently into the Indian Ocean off the Australian coast. Four months and counting of uninterrupted adventure on and off the bicycle, mostly on, had begun to take its toll. This time there'd be no crying wolf, no bracing for the impact or dressing it up in flowery superlatives. This time it felt as if I'd rolled right up to the edge of the world and had little equilibrium left to avoid a nasty fall. So I did the only smart thing I could think of, which was to sit my tired arse down.

Resting on dusty and scuffed elbows in the half-light along one of Perth's spectacular beaches, I pondered the rougher edges of existence, examining it as best I could for a guy who'd emerged from thousands of miles of cycling the forsaken and forgotten places of the world.

What to do once you've toured purgatory on a bicycle and found it something of a showstopper? A twisted little spot deep in my core was actually going to miss navigating through the world's largest kiln and blackfly preserve. Long before *Forrest Gump* popularized a similar idea on-screen, I seriously considered touching my front tire into the Indian Ocean, then turning around and heading back the way I came, crisscrossing that Down Under continent over and over—Indian, Pacific, Indian, Pacific—until I outpaced my own skin, achieved nirvana, or perished trying.

I'd left one side of a damn wide continent in a complete sprint, a blind-with-fury dive into the desert. It had become abundantly clear to me that God was out to lunch, deaf, or worse. This wouldn't have upset me as much if I'd worn a lot of black during my formative years and really listened to the lyrics of the Cure, but I'd been an unfailingly optimistic chap to that point. Existential angst should be dished out in manageable bites, not dropped on your head like those anvils in the Road Runner cartoons. So I was as surprised as a jumper whose chute hadn't opened to be standing on the ground in nearly one piece. Granted, if you attempt to burn yourself clean of vague imperfections through aimless velocity, chances are you're gonna suffer some collateral damage. At that moment, I felt rather wrung out, thin as origami paper, and just plain beat.

The sun was halfway under now. If a man were quick enough, or maybe it's more a matter of purity and focus than outright speed, could that man slip the seam between heaven and earth, between dying light and rushing water— eye of the needle, effortlessly, and emerge somewhere unsullied and substantial? I craved substance like a baby reaches out for mother's milk. Maybe my days came down to pedaling after mirages, always chasing something in the distance, spinning away my youth. Once you start wrestling with the premise of ceaseless adventure as a career choice, things can get dicey.

Close enough to touch, the sun would be gone in another instant. I started to focus all of my kinetic energy, willing some part of me to follow it over the lip of the world, but an annoying high-pitched, mechanized hum distracted me. A final flicker of light, and my metaphysical escape—white boy from the 'burbs seeks a higher plane of consciousness— was out of reach for another day. I was such a wreck at that point I couldn't even appreciate the inherent comic value in that image.

At least the sand made a decent pillow. When I could be bothered to open my eyes again, I was staring at the hairy kneecap of a kilt-wearing man covered in cartoon-size muscles. He was revving a light blue Vespa—an Italian-made moped with wide metal gills fanning across its front. That rather familiar mechanized hum sputtered to a stop beside my loaded bicycle. First thought: Who in their right mind would rev a Vespa? Said scooter would cause me untold misery over the next few days, but at that moment it looked innocent enough—toylike, even. The same could not be said for its bodybuilding driver. In addition to the kilt, this grinning Scotsman was sporting a tight black leather jacket cut off at the sleeves and open down the middle. This revealed a T-shirt with the words "In Case of Rapture, I'll Be Busy Looting the Homes of the Righteous." He got off his ride and stood almost directly over me.

While nirvana had escaped me, from that angle I was dangerously close to finding out if Kilt Man was wearing anything under his traditional garb. Tired as I felt, I sprang to my feet and offered a grin and a nod. You have to give it up for such a healthy skepticism of organized religion, to say nothing of his daring, if misguided, fashion sense. He looked like the love child of Arnold Schwarzenegger and Cyndi Lauper.

"I take it by your getup that this isn't a quick wheel down to the store for a pint of milk," he said.

Technically, the words that formed when he spoke were English, but try to imagine the voice of Sean Connery spliced together with that of Crocodile Dundee. Now multiply by four, carry the remainder, drop half your consonants, and then you'd be in the ballpark.

I felt fairly confident he was talking about my bike and some sort of food purchases, but it could just as easily have been a proclamation regarding land reparations in South Wales. When in doubt, my traveler's sixth sense kicks in. Normally I'd fall back on current events or the weather for conversation topics, but since I'd been in the outback for weeks, I had very little idea what was going on in the world, and only a moron would point out that it was going to be a warm, clear night again.

"I've just come across the Nullabor Plain," was the best I could deliver.

"Insanity," he stated.

I understood that well enough.

"True, but in my case just what the doc ordered."

He nodded. "Ah, well, we all have to take our medicine, don't we?"

It was like learning pig Latin or tuning in a cheap boom box whose antennae had snapped off years ago.

"Donny." He extended a hand.

"Joe." I met his fierce grip.

"You want to go round for a bite?" Donny asked.

But what I heard was, "You want to go run for a bit?"

I declined, explaining that I run only when the police are chasing me. Besides, I was too thoroughly beat for any more real exercise.

The bulky heathen frowned a second. "Lock your bike and bring your bags—we can take my Vespa." He patted the seat of his moped and tossed me a helmet. I tapped my helmet and tossed his back. So began my verbally impaired friendship with this wild Scottish Aussie of the western shores of Oz. I locked up and, Lord help me, climbed aboard that buzzing blue devil.

Zipping about in unsteady fashion through the streets of Perth on the back of a blue Vespa is a rare privilege. As I clung feverishly to the leather jacket of a man clothed in what amounted to a skirt, it never even crossed my mind that maybe I *had* managed to escape my reality, slip that seam after all. Too tired and frightened to ponder it further, I was just glad not to be pedaling for once.

Donny favored me with a comprehensive Vespa tour of the city when all I really craved was protein. Eventually Donny's own stomach overruled his civic pride; he stopped incoherently shouting out landmarks and allowed that we should find a little place for some grub.

"The skirt is heritage, something to be proud of, sure, and it's my business alone if I want to work, sleep, and drink in this getup, but the truth is I sport it only a few times a year. I'm planning to squat the week at the Highland Games is all." Donny tore away at another section of a meaty sandwich. He'd been gripping the roll tightly enough that I'd have sworn rigor mortis was setting in. Each bite reminded me of a lion ripping into a freshly killed antelope. He nodded in approval of his dinner. For all of his confusing exterior, Donny seemed to know exactly who he was.

"The clans gather in Lathlain Park once a year. It's a nice spot of ground up the road a hop. You're quite welcome to join me. Sheepdog shows, caber tossing, footraces, and plenty of bagpipes."

The accent was getting easier to understand. It had a definite rhythm and spike to it, and once I connected the dots and heard some words a few times . . . well, I'm no code breaker, but he was tuning in better. And my blood sugar had climbed back up onto the charts—maybe that had something to do with it as well.

"As much as I love the sound of bagpipes across an open field, Donny, I think I need to stretch out on the beach for a couple hundred years and detox from my outback adventure. I do remember attending some Highland Games in Pittsburgh when I was a kid. Good times. They had bagpipes as well," I noted.

"Bagpipes? Let me tell you something about a Scotsman's pipes." Donny exuded an endless supply of optimism coupled with an easygoing ability to ignore what he didn't want you to have said, extracting only what he felt he needed from your statements. After that, Donny simply massaged that into any story he wanted to tell. Come to think of it, his technique resembled the bulk of my own career as a journalist.

"A guy is lucky to be playing pipes today and not hundreds of years ago. See, if a Scotsman heard bagpipes blowing in the distance, it meant that a war party would be descending on his clan any moment, looking to cause serious damage. You know, Mel Gibson in *Braveheart*-level mayhem. The piper usually got his hands cut off to send a message back to these aggressors that they were walking into a world of hurt."

Donny's sweet little tale of the piper's plight made me question why anyone would have taken up the bloody instrument voluntarily back then.

"Today the worst punishment a piper receives is maybe a noise violation from the authorities when someone phones in a public complaint." Donny finished off his sandwich, and finally his fingers relaxed. "What most people don't realize is that the sound of pipes on the morning air always brings with it a reckoning of some sort."

Donny's history lesson did jog loose a memory of melancholy bagpipes, a gorgeous string of musical moments at the end of a funeral held for a good friend of my father's. After the service, Dad drove my brother and me, teenagers in Florida at the time, out to the airport, where we stood on the roof of the parking garage, evening shadows growing large as we counted plane after plane break the bounds of gravity and Doppler into the next time zone. Dad said nothing when we popped a couple of his tallboys and drank them in the open. He just stared at the distant horizon, quietly humming what sounding like part of that piper's melody now and then. I watched him watch planes until I lost his tired, textured face in the shadows of dusk.

When Donny deposited me safely back at the beach, it felt like I was letting him down.

"Sure you won't change your mind?" he asked.

Rarely did I pass on a party, especially one that promised grown men dancing in plaid dresses and throwing large, unwieldy objects over high bars and into pits of sand. And Donny, he was something of a grand sideshow of the highest magnitude, with or without a Scottish Highland shindig on his agenda.

"Maybe I'll catch up with you, ride out to the games in a few days." I said this with enough conviction to make it sound like a real possibility, except I knew it to be nothing more than pleasant chatter. I needed more time to ease back into the world, to incrementally fill in the silence of the outback rather than smack myself around too badly with a rowdy week of Highland Games.

It must have been an hour later when I bolted to my feet, kicking sand as I rose. That sickening feeling of loss vibrated from the back of my ankles to the top of my head, heating it to a brain-baking burn until I resembled a lit cigarette. When rifling through my gear for the third time failed to produce my wallet, I paused and took a deep breath. My bike fell over and the rear wheel spun slowly in the darkness. During this failed effort to center myself, I tried emulating all those poised people you see in commercials for international-style coffees. I thought about Adirondack chairs and cotton shirts blowing gently in the breeze, of early morning fog over a placid lake, and Sunday afternoons stretched out in a hammock while dressed in designer labels. When I returned from my brief, Madison Avenue–sponsored vacation, my wallet was still missing. The process of beating my head on a cement post near a seawall seemed like the next logical course of action.

During fifty thousand miles of pedaling I'd never as

much as let my billfold out of my sight. Now it was buzzing down a road dangerously close to the exposed plumb-
ing of an excitable Scotsman. My recollection of events
was hazy, but hadn't I placed it under the seat of the Vespa
as we tore out on our city tour? He had no idea he had my
wallet and might not look under the seat for days. Small
miracles, my passport, and a healthy chunk of traveler's
checks were tucked safety into my left pannier, but that
wallet contained a wad of always-needed cash, ID, and,
most crucial, addresses and phone numbers of cherished
friends I'd made throughout New Zealand and Australia.
Hold the phone—hadn't I also slipped my plane ticket in
there earlier that day? I'd been studying the times and
connections to help plan out my next move. But clearly my
next move was decided now. Instead of recharging on the
beach, I had to chase down one bulky Scotsman on a blue
Vespa. He had a working motor and over an hour's head
start, so there was no hope I'd catch him along the blacktop. This meant I'd be attending those Highland Games
after all.

"Doesn't ring a bell," said the proper-looking woman
holding back a sheepdog the size of a small barge. "But then
you'll need more of a description for the man than that. As
you can see, the grounds are crawling with lads in kilts. Have
a bash at it, for what good it will do you, but do come back
around for the dog show—it's first-rate or I didn't organize it."

She was right, of course. Donny, who would attract
attention at anything short of New York's Halloween parade, didn't stick out at all in this crowd—a realization that
wasn't helping my mood any. I'd already labored for the

better part of the morning, pedaling farther and farther away from the beach, only to be confronted by my worst-case scenario: a sea of plaid kilts and a massive assortment of energetic folk, from happy hooligans half lit before the noon hour to families in campers making a long weekend or a full-fledged vacation out of the event. There must have been in the neighborhood of a thousand noisy souls moving about the grounds. I wandered through the parking fields for a while, but if the blue Vespa was stashed out there, it was well hidden.

The festival did not have an official lost-and-found area, as far as I could tell. But before I could ask many questions at the info booth, a crush of patrons forced me into this merry stream of humanity. I was carried past tables and along a midway of ticky-tacky craft displays. Everyone seemed hell bent on finding a seat for the Scottish country dancing performance, so I darted for a place beside them, sort of like musical chairs without the music. All this time I hadn't thought of myself as a lemming, but the evidence was damning. I perched on my chair in anticipation of . . . whatever these other people were excited about. At least it might take my mind off my wallet for a moment.

It wasn't five minutes into the dance performance when tears started running down my face. I would love to defend my emotions by telling you that the dancers were so exquisite, it was akin to witnessing an act of God's grace displayed through agility and perfect timing, dresses woven from angel's wings, and smiles that burned brighter than the midday sun. But in reality it was a second-rate talent show performance by locals clearly enjoying themselves but not tuning up for their Broadway debut by any means.

No, what laid me low was the pure, unfettered exuberance of one young boy as he spun and jumped awkwardly about. When had I stopped feeling like that? For such a long time the act of riding my bicycle had held back the weight of the world, but gravity was finally winning, and I couldn't or wouldn't deal.

I wandered around the festival for a while like an extra in a zombie movie, shuffling from exhibit and booth, pawing merchandise for no purpose and making halfhearted attempts to keep scanning for Donny and my wallet. I even let someone paint a traditional family crest on my cheek at the free face-painting booth.

"You want a toss?"

This request, made by a hulking mass of a man holding a heavy lead ball, barely registered with me, but his pencil-thin mustache was certainly a curiosity. I studied his upper lip as the man continued to speak.

"Mate, you look like someone stole your pudding."

Pudding? If only it was pudding.

I launched into my story, condensing things a bit but hitting the highlights so he would fully appreciate my mood. The kindness in his eyes was so comforting that the comments that followed stunned me.

"Come on now, don't be such a nancy boy. You're young, you look healthy enough, and you're seeing the world on your own terms, if I understand you right. Get it together, mate. Get it to-bloody-gether."

Clobbering me with one of those huge cabers would have hurt less. But he wasn't finished yet.

"You're overthinking the deal. It happens—not to guys like me, but it happens. Letting your brain load you down like that isn't useful. If I were you, I'd throw something heavy."

Who the hell was this guy to give me advice?

So I threw something heavy.

Then I tossed something else. And more things, and then I moved over to the fifty-pound balls over the high bars. I kept tossing things right through lunch. That's when they showed me how to lift the caber hammer properly. At more than a hundred pounds, you don't want that thing getting away from you and taking out a corps of pipers warming up for the afternoon march. If I learned nothing else about that hammer, I discovered that it requires proper adult supervision.

"Look, we could use another strong back for our next tug-of-war heat."

Even I knew this to be an honor. I rushed to my place somewhere in the middle of the line. Another truck posing as a lad gave me a pair of gloves, showed me how to distribute my weight, and explained why it was important not to regrip the rope unless you kept solid, even tension going with the other hand. I was so engrossed in practicing that I barely looked at the opposing team, or my own mates for that matter.

I didn't hear Donny's incoherent mutterings until after the whistle blew. His efforts sounded like a blue whale in heat, but I would have recognized that incoherent speech pattern of his anywhere. Turned out he was the anchor man on the opposing team. I thought about Donny's girth, flashed back to how he'd held on to his sandwich, and reckoned we were in trouble.

"Donny boy!" I hollered.

"Joe?"

I guess it was just enough of a distraction, hearing my Yankee voice on the other side of the rope. Whatever the reason, we had the advantage from that point forward. They put up a ferocious fight, and gloves barely kept my hands from bleeding out, but in the end Donny went arse over teakettle with the rest of them.

"You had enough of the beach, then," Donny surmised. But what I heard him say was, "You had to eat the bitch hen." It was going to take some time to tune back in to Donny's frequency. But it was great to see him. Oh, was it great to see him.

Nothing seemed to be able to shake my recently elevated mood, even the news that my wallet was not inside the Vespa. For all I knew, dingos had eaten it just outside of Kalgoorlie.

"What are you going to do?" asked Donny.

"Ah, it'll sort out." And I sincerely believed, for the first time in a long while, that it would. I looked up at Donny and nodded. "Right now, though, I think I'd like to throw a few more really hefty items, maybe that hammer deal again."

Donny offered a wide grin.

"Good on ya."

━━ ━ ━━

Life gives away its secrets begrudgingly, in fits and starts, if at all. But here's one truth that's held, and a good thing, too, because I had to pedal halfway around the world to locate it.

When burdens are crushing you, when it all gets to be

too much to shoulder, why not try throwing something heavy? You'd be surprised.

But remember: Always stretch, bend at the knees, and for God's sake, whatever you do, don't start with that big hammer the man over there in the funny-looking kilt is tossing around.

THE ECONOMY OF MOVEMENT
(HOW I FOUND
AND LOST THE GLIDE)

Beyond the brightly colored clamor of Puerto Vallarta's *mercados*, past the carnivalesque barking of time-share ropers and the beachfront Grand Prix, past the battered taxis and buses jockeying for purchase along tight cobblestone streets, beyond all the sand, sloth, and *cerveza*, stood the jungles of Jalisco, Mexico. Those towering ridges on the near horizon whisper greetings and a veiled challenge atop the humid breeze: "*Hola*, Metal Charro. Bring what you have, city boy, and hope it gets you over."

Drifting peacefully through the womblike waters of the Gulf of Baja, I offered a cocky nod in the direction of those looming slopes. An empty gesture. I had no idea what the cloud forests held.

I tried placing a call to my folks before I set off into the deep bush, but I couldn't get an outside line. Normally I would have waited until I was back in the country to chat with my parents, but I'd just gotten the news that a bit of prostate cancer had surfaced, so Dad was going to start elective treatments. I wanted to cheer him up, take his mind off the nasty realities of life. Thanks to him, I'd been on summer vacation most of mine. Not that he funded my days as an adult, but it had been through his example of grinding it out for a callous corporation that I'd been shown what I did not want to do with my days. Conventional as his life was, Dad always seemed to find real joy in hearing me describe the setting and cast of characters of my latest adventure. I'd try again on the other side of the trip.

A brief plane ride in a creaky old Buddy Holly special and a dicey landing deposited us and the bikes onto a gravel strip surrounded by a sprawling canopy—a bold green latticework of tight vines and plants, spiders the size of pinwheels, butterflies as wide as fruit bats, and some of the most outrageous climbs and technical downhill pedaling south of the border. I shook my head, fearing that the jungle had my number.

The group, a baker's dozen of varying endurance and skill levels, had separate agendas or lack thereof. An incomplete snapshot included Samantha and Roger, a dotcom couple sinking their efficient teeth into what would most likely be transitory wealth; Jon, a stressed-out CEO turned stressed-out, but less so, pool cleaner. He danced swing on the weekends to shake loose the convulsions of nervous energy he couldn't pedal away on the trails; Terry, an undercover DEA officer months from retirement, sort of an anti–Don Johnson in look and style, a sweet, socially incapacitated man who drank early and hard, but maybe that was his cover; a divorcee checking her lip gloss in the bike mirror every few miles; marketing executives being marketing executives—in the jungle, for Chrissake; a couple in comfortable denial at the dimming dream that was their marriage; and an aerospace engineer who needed to be first on the plane, into the hotel, onto the trail. In short, good folks at something of a loss as to when their lives had gotten so damn far away from them.

I was familiar with this feeling. I've tried, with uneven success, to dodge such bullets by never presuming my grip on the wheel is as tight as I think. The illusion of control is a wicked little parlor trick. My own agenda involved no more than chasing a bit of time out of mind in pursuit of adrenaline and maybe a new story or two for the campfire. I'd leave with something more valuable and lasting, coveted even: object lessons in the economy of movement.

Alejandro and Chiquis waited placidly at a switchback halfway up a windswept, eroding mountain. These were my tutors, patient gents. Alejandro was Jalisco's top off-road racer, a wisp of a man who used his unthreatening exterior like a secret weapon. He'd carried the national title a few years back. That's the yellow jersey for all of Mexico, sports fans. Chiquis called himself a road racer who'd turned his attention to dirt in recent years. Built like an army bunker, he had the most pleasant speaking voice I'd ever heard. While the rest of us shuttled by plane to the start point, Chiquis had pedaled the uphill gauntlet ahead of the sag vehicle, using it as a sunrise warm-up ride. Both guys were nipping at thirty, though they looked barely old enough to buy beer. I had yet to hear labored breathing from either quarter. This sort of nonchalant talent would have annoyed me if they'd worn it as badges, but for both men it wrapped around them like second skins.

The economy of movement loosely defined: This is not

about crunching numbers in a bland industrial park cubicle, and while it may involve slowing down on the bicycle to shred faster in the long run, it is something beyond the realm of speed. The economy of movement depends on riding with purpose, conservation of power, and decisiveness—changing the way you approach the trail and yourself. It's allowing restraint to pick the cleanest line down a boulder-strewn hillside and trusting forward motion, force of will, conditioning, position, and more restraint to clear a blisteringly technical uphill—places where donkeys fear to tread. Once you embrace and master the economy of movement, you appear to float over gravel and glide past riders pushing three times as hard and weaving east and west so as not to dump their bikes.

Another benefit to the economy of movement that Alejandro pointed out, "*Más kilómetros* left in the legs."

We took a short break under some avida trees, a pitiful attempt to retreat from the brutal heat of October near the equator. I'm told the wide leaves were fed to Montezuma to exact his now famous intestinal revenge. I declined a sample.

"Only m-m-mad dogs and Englishmen go out in the m-m-midday sun," our host, Bobby Lampaert of B-B-Bobby's Bikes, quoted Kipling with a Cheshire-cat grin.

An incredibly likable guy, B-B-Bobby knew the mountains better than any white man in Jalisco. Arguably he was a more learned guide than most of its native sons and daughters. To hear B-B-Bobby talk about the tours was to listen to a man in love with a time and place. "Guiding a jungle single-track tour in Mexico requires quite an attention span. From Chacala, Jalisco, you descend two thousand feet in just under six miles on the way to Yelapa along Banderas Bay's southern shore. Tropical rain ruts deep as a school bus limit your choices. Huge green-and-red parrots make a glorious racket as rays of sun pierce through the canopy. You really don't ever want it to end until you remember those shrimp tacos and cold beers waiting on the beach, and the stories you're gonna tell each other before a *panga* [boat] takes you and the bike back to Puerto Vallarta. The look on yet another first-timer's face as he clears the jungle is priceless. We try to do it once a week. I've had worse jobs."

B-B-Bobby had turned a slight stutter into his trademark and a marketing tool for his touring company. "When I want to lighten up the overly PC c-c-rowd on a tour, I'll s-s-ell them some bug spray. They always ask about the chemicals, and I tell them with a straight face, 'Except for a slight s-s-stammer in some users, it w-w-works like a charm.' " Though not a servant to anything with the word *economy* in its name (he'd been a roadie and sound man for the band Blood, Sweat, and Tears, for Pete's sake), B-B-Bobby understood the concept well enough to have hired Alejandro and Chiquis. Watching them tune up bikes and double back to check on stragglers, it was my suspicion they would have guided us into the jungles for close to nothing, just to be able to float and glide a while longer.

━━■━■━━

The economy of movement in practice:

The day was as relentless as it was grueling—four hours of steep climbing without a switchback in sight. It was similar in pace and pain to marching through a bog in Maine. I actually lost a bike shoe in a bog in the north woods, and when the bog takes your shoe . . . let it go, baby, it's gone. But taking on Mexico's high country had its rewards— a stunning view from La Bufa, seven thousand feet above the banana plantations and coffee trees, with a panoramic glimpse of the shoreline for starters. We were swing dancers and software consultants, physical therapists and that narcotics agent months away from early retirement, finding ourselves for a spell, sweating and huffing and gutting B-B-Bobby's fleet of specialized full-suspension bikes to the top.

Before Chiquis dropped me for good around hour two, I studied his form and tried to emulate it. He rode smart and steady, but there was more to it—a secret fuel source that didn't come with my operating model, something about his demeanor that superseded skills acquired at places like Dirt Camp and Fat Tire Festival. There was focused power and forward lean as though he were being pulled up the grade on unseen strings. His rear never came out of the seat unless it absolutely had to, and his shifting was almost supernatural in its anticipation, but barely audible. Chiquis's cadence was high and deliberate while never forcing the back wheel to slide out from under him, and I noticed that his arms stayed surprisingly loose and casual, like a pickpocket in a crowd. When he scanned around it was with fluid motions, catlike.

More and more I thought of him and Alejandro as *los gatos.* Transferring this image onto myself was no small feat, but for a few miles it worked. I detected the hint of a glide, started to grin, then my front wheel caught an edge and I was spending energy all over the place just to shift my way clear, pedal out of the wash, and get back onto the single track. In the meantime Chiquis had floated away.

━━━━

It would have been easy to wheel right by Christy's and never have known it was there. A little eatery in the village of San Sebastian, where electricity is a recent arrival, Christy's had a petite wooden sign over the door as the only clue that here was more than a humble residence. Inside, though, Christy's was a secret garden of sorts: open-air courtyard dining among the poinsettias with parrots cursing in Spanish if you didn't pay them enough attention. And the best beans and hot plates on the continent, spiked with lard and poppies, or some secret ingredient that made you want to tell the world at large how much you loved it.

To get there we had to hold on through twelve miles of uninterrupted ear-bleeding, shake-and-bake downhill riding. Even Mark, an Australian photographer with movie-star good looks and a religious fervor for speed and danger, called it enough. It was the type of riding that, if you live, works up a Texas-size appetite.

When someone in our party announced their vegetarian status, Christy, wearing eighty years of life in fine fashion, clucked her tongue and shared an expression of deepest pity, as if she'd been told they were dying of cancer or had just lost the use of a limb. "Why ride those bikes so much if not to enjoy your food?" Statues of the Virgin Mary smiled down as we cleaned our plates.

I pondered over the selections on Christie's jukebox for far too long. Mark, an expatriate of the Fatal Shore, swooped in and explained in his endearing Aussie accent that after five years in Mexico he'd finally clued to the fact that every jukebox in the country contained the same three songs played by a nameless mariachi band.

"Just put in your money and pick at random. I wouldn't be surprised if the blooming thing only holds one record and a drumbeat machine that changes the tempo once in awhile."

The charm of the country seemed to have worn off for Mark. Still, he danced away the beans and rice with the rest of us, until the shadows cast down by the mountains dictated our departure. Christy's parrots sang out "Go to hell, amigos" in two languages as we exited.

———————

Our next stop was a night lounging around a two-hundred-year-old Spanish villa, once the stomping grounds of famed director John Huston. I was informed that the table we'd propped our bruised legs upon was the very same where Huston and Tennessee Williams hammered out rewrites to the script for *Night of the Iguana*. Candles and hurricane lanterns provided the only light—enough to see the photos of movie stars such as Liz Taylor and the like watching over us.

Now and then peacocks called out from the yard. This was a perfect setting to dig into the heart of things. But when I pressed Alejandro and Chiquis for riding specifics, they discussed their families instead and the importance of the pace of the community. My newfound friends covered the joys and trials of raising boys and the trick to balancing work, riding, and free time. We stayed up half the night.

I knew these guys, I was these guys . . . except they

rode like lightning-fast ghosts released from the rules of gravity and I was still an earthbound mortal with the occasional moment of clarity.

"People come down here, look around, and maybe think we're lazy," Alejandro said, shaking his head slightly in the half-light of a candle. "What they don't see is we put energy in other places. I don't want to rule the world, I want more to laugh and look and ride right through it . . . swoosh."

The economy of movement revealed:

It was our final day of single track at high altitude, a thirty-plus miler with the perfect mix of climbing, technical stretches, and raging descents. Better still was that as fatigue and falls had taken the wind out of a few of our most gonzo riders, I was finally hitting my stride, this being the curse and blessing of a lifelong road rider, a touring cyclist put to dirt on occasion. It's why by midday I found myself chasing Alejandro's rear wheel through river crossings so deep and unpredictable that if you eased up even slightly you were taking a bath. We paused at a mini waterfall spilling over the trail and waited for the others.

"This next bit is uphill and maybe a little rough," Alejandro announced. Translation: *I'll try to stay within the same time zone.*

We clipped back in, and a strange thing happened. At first I was watching Alejandro's choices and mimicking them, but as people began dropping back or stopping altogether, I cleaned a choppy riverbed of smooth stone using my own line and pulled alongside my tutor. He nodded and produced a cowboy-style yelp in my honor.

What I determined to be the secret of the glide had come to me under a full moon the evening before. Alejandro, Chiquis, and I were motoring an old truck into town for some chocolate and a chance to use the one phone, El Presidente's, to see if we could reach our wives. The night was bright as day as we motored through cornfields and inched over the potholes along dusty roads. Bathed in the harvest moon's glow, the Eagles' greatest hits rocking gently in the background and Alejandro passing around a little weed, I observed in my pals' unguarded smiles that to float and glide you must navigate your moments with gratitude . . . all of them.

There's lots of talk about riding fearlessly and dominating the space, but how many people actually get on the bicycle with a sense of authenticity and gratitude each time out? Not greeting-card gratitude. An appreciation for cycling as a way of life, a meditation—a vocation, even—is a damn noble and hard-fought place to arrive at. But until you can absorb the white noise and effortlessly shed the emotional and physical turbulence that creeps in, until you ride like it's the last time you'll ever own a pair of legs, then you're destined to watch the art and beauty known as the economy of movement pass you by.

If only it were that simple. I decided to eat dinner at the surfside restaurant where Chiquis worked for his dad. The thatched roof and colorful patio chairs couldn't mute the desperate pace my new friend was forced to run at all day. No glide to be found. He smiled over, but it was cut short by a sea of tourists flooding him with orders at the bar.

For Alejandro it wasn't a restaurant but a *mercado* at the airport.

"I have to listen to these people haggle with me for shot glasses and T-shirts, acting the whole time as if I got the stuff for free and they're doing me a favor parting with a few pesos."

I paid full price for my trinkets and left, trying to reconcile the *el gato,* Buddha-like being I'd pedaled beside days ago with the man at the register straightening little pieces of wood carved to look like fish.

Hours before I left the country B-B-Bobby led me on a short ride. He wouldn't tell me where we were going, and I must have seemed anxious that I'd miss my flight.

"I know that feeling," B-B-Bobby said out of the blue. Roadie, sound man, and now mind reader. "You're on the back end of an adventure, and it's hard not to head home inside your head."

We climbed a tight thistle- and thorn-laden path in silence. I really wanted to be anywhere but on the bike again. In a flash I had to brake hard or risk riding into a vast pool created by a roaring waterfall. B-B-Bobby was already in, working his way behind this massive curtain of gravity-induced rain. I dove in.

"Still th-th-thinking about that plane you have to catch?"

He knew I wasn't.

"You gotta tr-tr-try to enjoy yourself right u-u-up till it's over."

Was he talking to me or just reminding himself? His was such an easygoing approach that it didn't feel like B-B-Bobby was trying to teach me anything, just mentioning something we both might have overlooked otherwise.

I gave an "Amen, B-B-Bobby," but he'd already gone back underwater.

My father's heart stopped abruptly only a few weeks after I returned from Mexico. I'd been trying to explain the economy of moment to him the last time we spoke on the phone, jabbering about my theory, but what he really wanted to know about was the color of the leaves that far south in October. Do they change? And if the church bells in Vallarta's city square rang every hour. Whether I made sense to him much of the time, we knew that I'd always been on a semipermanent summer vacation for the both of us these many years.

Unfathomably, B-B-Bobby's expiration date came up only a short time later. Both men went in their sleep. B-B-Bobby's life had been one without convention, and my father's had been littered with it. I needed to know that my dad had enjoyed himself, but it was too damn late to ask. Funny how you can feel like you know a man's state of mind you've spent fifteen days with better than that of a loving and loyal guy who held your hand on the first day of school and shook it firmly on the last.

I didn't get on my bike for weeks, not until B-B-Bobby stuttered out from the corner of a dream, one of those vivid early morning shoots that slips in just before sleep lets you go for good. He was over by the grill at Christy's, heating up some tortillas in the late afternoon sun and smiling like he was holding a winning ticket.

"Chiquis and Alejandro, th-th-those bastards are still out r-r-riding," he announced, like I'd been there the whole time. I watched him flip and stack a heap of mouth-watering floured circles, making perfect work of each one.

"By the way, your dad's f-f-fine. He's over there tr-tr-trying to locate something new on the j-j-jukebox." B-B-Bobby laughed hard and followed it up with a wink. "We haven't t-t-told him yet."

I didn't even have to turn around to know that Pop was livin' large under the lazy sun. B-B-Bobby had never steered me off course before. My dad had given his days to the grindstone, to family, to so many other people. Now it was his turn to be on summer vacation.

I woke up clean and was on the bike before breakfast. Damn it if my glide hadn't stayed back in the jungle, though, maybe something to do with not clearing customs at the border. But a safe bet? I haven't earned that level of movement yet. Maybe I never will. Also, I have my suspicions that if you could glide every time you went out the door, well, you just might never come back.

But I'd had a taste, and it's made getting on the bike—any bike, anywhere—new again.

ABOUT THE AUTHOR

Joe Kurmaskie is the author of *Metal Cowboy* and has written for *Details*, the *Arizona Star*, *Oregon Cycling*, and *Midwest Bike*. He is a regular contributor to *Bicycling*, where his "Ask the Metal Cowboy" column appears. He lives in Portland, Oregon, with his wife and two sons.

The Metal Cowboy's First Ride

Joe Kurmaskie, dubbed the "Metal Cowboy" by a blind rancher he ecountered one icy morning in Idaho, has been addicted to the intoxicating freedom and power of the bicycle ever since he "borrowed" his big sister's banana-seat bike at the age of five. *Metal Cowboy* is Joe's debut collection of bicycle adventures. Ride with him as he climbs a tree to avoid the insistent pecking of a flock of geese in New Hampshire, tools around a motel parking lot in Utah with a touring group of Elvis impersonators, or fills in as a last-minute scarecrow in a North Carolina Halloween parade—and enjoy the freedom of a path well pedaled and a life less ordinary.

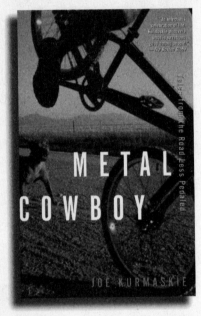

METAL COWBOY

0-609-80911-3
$13.00 paper (NCR)

"An infectious celebration of life. Kurmaskie uncovers what is sweet and good among people."
—Boston Globe